brushing
the tip
of fame

brushing the tip of fame

nicholas hope

BANTAM

SYDNEY • AUCKLAND • NEW YORK • LONDON

The names and personal characteristics of some individuals and organisations mentioned in this book, including the school attended by the author and any teacher referred to from that school, have been changed in order to protect their privacy. In these instances, any resemblance to organisations or to persons living or dead is entirely coincidental and unintentional.

First published in Australia and New Zealand in 2004
by Bantam

National Library of Australia
Cataloguing-in-publication entry

Hope, Nicholas.
Brushing the tip of fame.

ISBN 1 86325 440 4.

1. Hope, Nicholas. 2. Actors – Australia – Biography.
I. Title.

791.43028092

Transworld Publishers,
a division of Random House Australia Pty Ltd
20 Alfred Street, Milsons Point, NSW 2061
http://www.randomhouse.com.au

Random House New Zealand Limited
18 Poland Road, Glenfield, Auckland

Transworld Publishers,
a division of The Random House Group Ltd
61-63 Uxbridge Road, London W5 5SA

Random House Inc
1745 Broadway, New York, New York 10036

Typeset by Midland Typesetters, Maryborough, Victoria
Printed and bound by Griffin Press, Netley, South Australia
Cover design by Ellie Exarchos

10 9 8 7 6 5 4 3 2 1

This is my first book, so I'd like to dedicate it to Aesha, Rowena and Rachael.

prologue

The Question

I am so drunk the significance of the veiled telephone box escapes me. I don't even know where I am. The last two hours are something of a blur. There's a 1920s train, waitresses in what appears to be fetish gear serving free alcohol, a string quartet playing, a carriage full of people with unfamiliar Eastern European accents who are just as confused as me. I can see a small shop, the telephone box covered by a white sheet, other guests – guests? – staggering equally drunkenly up the hill.

Someone shouts: 'Look!' A television crew is arriving by helicopter. As it lands a crowd of local children attempt to jump up and touch the rotating blades. I can't work out what's going on.

Suddenly a large man with a dark moustache steps forward, waving his arms flamboyantly. He rips the sheet from the telephone box and opens the door. A white pigeon flies out and the television cameras raggedly follow it. The movement is too sharp for me. The flamboyant man disappears into the telephone box and his interpreter flatly addresses the intoxicated crowd. She tells us we are here for the opening of the first telephone box in the area. We are witnessing an historic event: the director of the festival is now making a phone call even as the homing pigeon we just saw wings its way to the same destination. We will see which is the faster service.

Director? I think. Festival? Yes! That's what it is! The Riga International Film Festival in . . . yes! Latvia! We were put on a train in Riga two hours ago for a secret festival surprise, and this town is it! I must be drunker than I thought, I'd forgotten for a while. There are smiles of relief on other faces around me as well. Perhaps the drinks were laced.

The phone call is taking some time and the crowd is getting restless. There is some trouble with the phone connection. There are fears the pigeon might win, but no, the director emerges triumphant. We all clap and cheer blearily. Riga Television films us to show how popular the event is, while locals look on distrustfully. We are dragged up the hill to have our photos taken with a wax sculpture of the iconic film director Sergei Eisenstein and to shake hands with the sculptor. This, we are told, is Eisenstein's home town.

It isn't.

I end up with my arms crossed in front of me, one hand shaking the sculptor's, the other holding Eisenstein's wax double. 'Smile Mr Bubby!' says the photographer, and I do. I can't think of any other response.

The smile is automatic and probably looks like a bad toothpaste ad, but the occasion is surreal and my head is swimming. As the flash goes off I see the camera image: a 35-year-old boy from Whyalla, South Australia, posing with a stranger and a wax dummy on a hill in the middle of Latvia, surrounded by sloshed critics, directors and actors from the struggling arthouse European filmmaking community. What am I doing here, when others are having their photos taken with the 'A' list of Hollywood? It seems an arbitrary and circuitous route to the kind of fame and fortune I think I want. But it is exotic and colourful.

'Mr Hope! Mr Hope! Quick quick, your interview, we must leave!'

I'm bundled into a car. The train has broken down and I have a press conference to attend. I explain to my Latvian translator that I may have trouble making sense, the alcohol . . .

'It's okay,' she says, handing me a bottle of clear liquid, 'just keep drinking.' I do.

The room's nearly spinning, but I manage to sit before I fall. There are garish colours and bright lights. From somewhere behind the lights – or is it in my head? – a voice repeats the question I was asked beside the wax Eisenstein.

'So, Mr Hope, what is it that has brought you here?'

The Answer

Bad Boy Bubby. That's what's brought me here. A film about an abused 35-year-old with limited verbal skills, a horror of the outside world, and an ability to mimic that enables him to survive once he has to leave the 'security' of his home.

I played Bubby.

The film won awards around the world, but it evaded blockbuster status and became a cult hit.

So did I.

That's why my fake smile ends up on the hill in Latvia, instead of featured on 'Entertainment Tonight'.

But I didn't know that when the film was first released. Back then, everything – ambition, hindsight, foresight – was still blurred, confused. There were festivals and parties in exotic locations and I was invited. Sometimes there were locked doors that hid famous celebrities, and sometimes I was on the inside. And there was always a lot of free booze. It felt really good, even if no one in my world saw it.

'And what made you choose that role, Mr Hope?'

They always ask that. The answer, of course, is because it was offered.

CHAPTER 1

being bubby

Audition, Adelaide, autumn 1992

'Have you been circumcised? I need to know.'

Writer/director Rolf de Heer is tall, gaunt, serious. He's sitting on the other side of the desk, he's considering me for the role of Bubby, and he wants an answer to his question.

My mind races.

I have read the first 20 pages of the script – they're the only ones written so far – and I know this is the kind of role people pray for. I don't know if I can do it, but that's immaterial. I can worry about that if I get it.

I've been brought in on the strength of my friend Tim Nicholls' short film *Confessor Caressor*, in which I play a wannabe rapist/murderer. There's no connection between the two roles as far as I can see, which impresses me. The tendency in filmmaking is to typecast. I've already been advised by a prominent local actor to present myself as a psychotic serial killer because I have the looks that could corner that market, and acting, says this actor, is all about cornering the market. But I don't want to be a psychotic serial killer. I want to be Bubby. He's an innocent and the centre of the film.

Since I don't know what answer Rolf wants, I tell the truth, which covers both eventualities. 'I'm not, but I look like I am.'

Rolf tells me it's all to do with authenticity. The character isn't supposed to have left his room. Circumcision suggests that he has. I think he's going to ask to have a look, and I've already resolved to let him, the casting couch is all his as far as I'm concerned – but he doesn't. Instead, he tells me more about the nature of the film. He doesn't expect it to be made for a while, money will be hard to get for such a project, he plans to shoot on weekends on out-of-date stock with whoever is in town, sound will be from microphones placed in the central character's wig, making it an aural point of view, and he is seriously considering me for the role if I am interested. I am. Desperately. But I'm about to go overseas for six months. 'That's not a problem,' says Rolf, 'there's no way we'll be ready to roll in six months. Leave a contact number and we'll keep you informed of developments.'

I am excited. I used to play in bands so I'm used to people promising things that never happen, but I'm still excited. Someone is considering me for the lead in an arthouse movie! It's more than I ever dreamt of when I left the Staff-Pay Department of Australia Post four years ago, after five years of working in a windowless office checking one set of documents against another to see if they matched. Five years spent avoiding the office manager who wanted me to wax my face because I didn't shave every day. Now I can go overseas, travel for four months in Europe, then two months in Africa.

I carry the 20 pages of script with me around the youth hostels of Europe. I don't read them, I don't want to jinx anything, but I like knowing they are there. Just before leaving the UK for Africa, I phone my parents in Adelaide. 'Nicholas,' says my mother, 'you'd better ring that director. You're in *TV Week*. They're starting that film, and they can't find you.'

Adelaide, spring 1992

Have you ever been to Adelaide? Funny place. Very flat, with wide streets. You notice this because there's nobody on them. A million people live in this city, but it's hard to tell where they all are.

As I fly in, I see the parklands that ring the city centre, the legacy of an architect who some say also designed prisons. The parks created a space between North Adelaide, set on a slight rise and equivalent to the officers' quarters, and Adelaide city, down below and set out in a prison-like grid system. Adelaide was the first non-convict city to be established in Australia, and many of the older, moneyed inhabitants are proud of this distinction. We circle over various suburbs that spread out towards the western coast, the northern desert, the eastern hills, and the southern Great Ocean Road. Their gentle sprawl belies the fact that Adelaide and its environs have been the location of a startling number of grisly, and often unsolved, serial killings.

This is home. This is the place where I feel safe. I know how this place works. My parents pick me up, as excited about the film as I am, and it's comforting. There's just a little bit of nagging guilt, that fear that was there in the first interview – *I don't know if I've actually got what it takes to do the part.* And I don't know how to get it.

The first noticeable thing about film is how easy every-thing becomes. My car is unregistered – the company will see to the registration. I haven't had time to shop for food – food will be provided at the office. I am out of money –

they will advance me part of the first week's wages. I need to sort out my banking and look for somewhere to live – they will drive me around, scour the papers for adverts, make some of the calls for me while I rehearse. All the stress of life is taken away. I become bubbly and childlike. I'm surprised at how quickly it becomes normal to live like this.

I love it. I love it so much, I decide to involve myself in all the facets of the film. Surely that'll help me develop my character. I go and look over the plans and construction of the film studio, which is being transformed into the two-room slum the character lives in. The plans don't make that much sense to me, but I fake it as best I can. The man who's drawing them wants suggestions. He believes I've spent the last four months thinking about this. I haven't, but I don't want to disappoint him, or get a bad reputation so early. So I just agree with everything he says. Do I think some ledges in the wall would be good as leverage for leaping into the air? Yes! Absolutely! And what do I think about putting bars across the ceiling to hang from? Great idea! And perhaps a kennel-like thing in the corner that I could sit in and poke my head out of? Fabulous! None of it gets approved in the end, but we're both happy agreeing on it. And I'm discussing all this in a film studio! Who would've thought?

I enter into lengthy discussions with the ex-ASIO man who is building mini-microphone transmitters that will be sewn into my wig. Ex-ASIO. They've got an ex-secret-service guy working on this. And he's really meek and mild, a bit like the torturer in the film *Brazil*. He's hand-making the equipment – it's probably based on surveillance gear used by the secret service, but he won't say. He's still bound by the Official Secrets Act, or something like that. It's all so different to theatre, it's so disparate, and it's all focused around the character I will play.

I try to learn about camera technique. How different lenses affect the size of performance. It seems pretty easy, really. Big lenses make you big and small lenses make you small. A big movement when you're big looks huge, and so on. Stands to reason, but Ian the cameraman talks very solemnly about it. He thinks there are a limited number of actors who understand the technique. I think maybe I've got a good chance. If I just stay small all the time it'll look really subtle.

Now that I've got the camera work nailed, I visit the accountant to enquire about the budget. I find out that it hasn't arrived, that my rehearsal pay of $300 a week is the result of other people delaying their own payments. The film has been promised all its money but hasn't received any cash flow as yet. At $800,000 it is very low budget, especially for a nine-week shoot on 35-millimetre film. But there is some dispute or 'lack of understanding' between the Italian producer, Domenico Procacci, and the Film Finance Corporation, who are both sharing the financing. I'm beginning to develop such a loyalty to the film that I'm almost tempted to give the money back, until the accountant tells me she's surprised any actor would agree to do the role so cheaply.

I start to worry that I have undersold myself, and that

people are laughing behind my back. Then she shows me the budget, and I realise all the actors are working for the same daily or weekly rate. No one is laughing.

Still, I don't give the money back. Rolf tells me not to. He tells me that he has budgeted for me to hang around the production office for a week or two, so the project will become more familiar to me. He's even decided to involve me in the casting process.

It's not much fun. We're nearly as nervous as the people who audition. There are these awkward pauses, where we all wonder what to say. Rolf appears uncomfortable with small talk, so the 'how are you?'s are mine to ask. And I know the answer already, I know everyone is lying. The correct answer is: 'I'm nervous as hell and I've got 15 minutes to convince you to put me in a feature film and I'm trying to guess what it is you want.' But the stated answer usually goes: 'Fine thanks, how are you?', which leaves everyone where they were before. At any rate, we manage to bumble through our meetings, despite one man being so upset at not being cast that he sends violent threats via my agent. Rolf sighs. 'It happens,' he says. 'Don't worry.' I do.

I'm beginning to worry a lot. We've started rehearsals, and Rolf's allowed me to conduct a number of theatre games to establish status relationships between characters, which he has taken part in. At one point I get really excited and order him to wash my feet and then drink the water. It's a master–servant set-up, it's supposed to help us get into the feel of subservience and rebellion. But afterwards, when he's left, in a hurry, I get concerned that maybe I'm overstepping the mark, pushing the relationship too far. It's too late, though – I've already organised a '60s-style Nude Day with Rolf, me and the actresses I'm going to spend the most nude time with, to desensitise us all to our nakedness. When Rolf doesn't turn up it's just me and the women. I worry.

But the film's preparation escalates each day, and my excitement grows with it. The set is being constructed, the crew is gathering, costumes are being prepared, roles are being cast, and I'm a part of all of it. The wig is turning into a prop as the microphones, transmitters and aerials are sewn into it to allow sound to be recorded directly from my head. The best system for picking it up turns out to be two car radios with coat-hanger aerials. I practise with it each day, learning how to turn to pick up relevant sound.

'We'll credit you as actor and boom swinger,' says Rolf. 'You can be the world's first binaural actor.'

I don't know what a boom swinger is and I don't know what binaural means, but everything I hear is equally strange, equally exciting. Snippets of bizarre information reach me. A report that 200 garden snails have been released inside the studio-built slum to create 'positive vibes'. A rumour that the walls of the slum have been smeared with semen for visual and energy enhancement. An overheard story that the guitarist from The Police has read the script and wants to act in the film. This whole thing just grows, day by day. And I'm the centre of it!

The Italian-based producer, Domenico, turns up one day from Rome with a contingent of Armani-clad companions, and takes us all to dinner. Their English isn't very good, and none of us speaks Italian. A journalist translates. Domenico listens to my ideas about the film and the character. I am so cosmopolitan, so in control.

And then, when the first day of filming comes, I collapse internally. Remember the first day of school? How exciting the new school clothes were, and the new shiny shoes, and the books and pencils and the pencil case? And then suddenly you have to go there! I realise I'm unprepared. I'm used to testing the wig, playing theatre games, observing cats, crawling on acrobat mats, flirting with the female staff. Now I have to act. I don't even have a finished script, let alone a character. There's a whole section that has to be rewritten, where Bubby meets some children with cerebral palsy and assists them in a school performance. None of the parents of the children will allow them to be in the film. They find the script obscene. Rolf is thinking of using the adults he's met at the Cerebral Palsy Centre but has no idea how to incorporate them into the story. And we're about to start shooting. I'm sick with fear.

The first two hours are taken up with make-up, and wig and microphone fittings, including tuning in to the radio. I struggle to keep calm and friendly as people fiddle with my head. Fred the microphone man takes forever to adjust the frequency and volume of the transmitters. He pokes away with miniature screwdrivers just above my ears and tests the results on the makeshift car radio receivers. He's been doing this for days. Why hasn't he got it right? I want to hit him. Make-up Beverly keeps readjusting the wig, pulling my natural hair through the lace and pushing hair clips into my scalp. It hurts. I want to hit her, too.

But at least it delays the first moment of filming. Until, finally, my screen mother, Claire, and I walk on set to rehearse the first shot of me being shaved. 'Show us what you'll do,' says Rolf, and I freeze. I cannot think of an interesting way to be shaved. I sit down and look up at Claire as she stands behind me and draws the fake razor over my face. I count to three, and jerk as if I have been cut, like it says in the script. I hope Rolf can help me here.

'Great!' he says, and we *film* it. Everybody is happy. James the soundman is ecstatic over the sound; Rolf is happy with the performance; Ian the cameraman is happy with the shot.

This is too easy. I know I'm faking. Either they'll find out when the developed film rushes are shown tomorrow, or they are amateurs. My stomach starts to knot. I missed out on a pre-paid tour of Africa for this, I've burnt a few bridges. The least people can do is help me look professional.

We move on.

For the next scene I have to stand naked in a tub of water as Claire washes me. I strip off and step into the little tub. The crew of 15 or so people are standing in the corner, with the camera, looking at me. It is a vulnerable moment. The focus puller walks over to measure the distance between me and the camera. Ian tweaks the lights. Claire shows how she intends to wash me. It takes a long time. The crowd in the corner makes me hyperaware of my nudity. I freeze up inside and try to imagine them out of existence. I'm annoyed that they haven't stripped off with me.

When Rolf calls 'Action!' and Claire begins to wash me, I am in a state of semi-coma. Claire raises my arm to wash under it, and I'm so stiff with nerves I forget to lower it afterwards. We do the shot a few times, but it's this first one that ends up in the film. It makes the character's morning routine look convincingly automated. So much for acting.

This first day defines my acting approach. I call it Smothering The Fear. I develop a technique of blanking out the camera and crew, focusing intently on the isolated task of each shot. It helps me get through the shooting and incidentally helps create the reality of Bubby's existence. It's a fortunate accident that's hard to re-create in later films, and one which suits the character's innocence and acceptance. It's also very Stanislavsky – 'The Actor Prepares'.

But I don't know this. For me, it's just a way of coping.

Filming, Adelaide, summer 1992/93

Filming is like most things. Believe me, you get used to it. And because a lead role takes up a lot of time, it becomes the main focus of your life. Its intensity allows it to become the only reality for a while, and that's comforting. Everything else becomes relatively pointless.

By the end of the first week I've found a place to live, or at least I've agreed on one of the places that has been found for me. Money is, by my standards, pouring in at $1000 a week less tax. I feel richer than I've ever been. We're going to have five weeks filming, a two-week break for Christmas, then another four weeks filming. It's like being on a train. I can't do anything else until the journey finishes. The sensation is divine.

But there's a downside. Although you may get used to the process of filming, it's not so easy to get used to being the focus of everyone's expectation. It's like this: everyone comes on to the set to watch how you are going to act the scene. It's early in the morning, the sun may not even be up, or maybe it's early evening and the sun is just setting. You haven't had a chance to really think about this – you may have thought through what the scene means and what you'd like people to get from it, but that's nothing compared with actually doing it. You're making it up on the spot and, generally, they're taking that as definitive and working on it. You go back to make-up while they drag walls out, set up lights all over the place, make space for the camera to move unhindered, rehearse how the camera will move – all on your first impressions of how you might do the scene. You are locked in, and by now you're doubting what you did. But you have to go back, an hour or two later, after they've fixed everything, and try to make those first bumbling decisions look convincing – and they're all expecting you to. And once you've done whatever you did, it's on to the next shot. You're stuck with it. And no one comes up to say 'that was bloody fantastic!'. Granted, no one comes up and says 'that was shit!' either, but that's what I suspect they must be thinking.

My ego is confused. I feel incompetent for the first week, especially after seeing the rushes. This should be harder – I should be living and dreaming the character, and I'm not. I go home at the end of each day, go through the next day's scenes, read a book or watch TV or look at my bank account. It doesn't seem right. At the end of that week, I drag Rolf aside and offer him the option of recasting me and starting again before it's too late. I'm convinced I'm faking and convinced it shows.

He looks at me as if I'm mad. He explains that, for this role, and up to this point in filming, he considers me as good as any actor he has worked with. He doesn't want to recast. He tells me he has even flirted with the idea of giving me a co-directing credit. I am shocked.

But boy am I flattered! It strikes me, he must be right. After all, he's made several films before this, he knows what he's talking about, yeah? I begin to get very cocky, and now this is exacerbated by being the centre of attention every day. Early on, the nature of every shot depends on what I do and how I do it, and the general idea on set is that the efficiency of my acting is affected by my mood. Everybody is nice to me; almost everybody defers to me. The whole set is arranged to accommodate me as comfortably as possible. Everything I say is listened to and acted upon. I see this as evidence that everyone thinks what Rolf thinks. It begins to go to my head, and there's a growing fight between my ego, which now knows it should be co-directing the show, and my desire to stay visibly humble so that everyone will like me. I begin to act like Dickens' Uriah Heep.

Other people's reactions to this evolving self are varied. One of the crew is in training. He is young, with cropped hair and a snake tattoo, and he is fascinated that I will be naked with several women throughout the film. He believes that this is something I will want to talk about each day. It isn't. There's a limit to how sexist I can appear to be, and how sexist I can appear to allow the film to be, and he's overstepping it. I want to tell him, and I want to tell him when other people are around so that they get to under-stand what a good guy I am. But he only brings up the naked women when he gets me on my own – it's meant to be that kind of male-buddy thing. I start to treat him with polite terseness in an attempt to create 'personal distance'. He accuses me of 'being a star'. It stings, until – bonanza! One of the women complains to Rolf about the boy's lewd comments. She has to sing a song while attaining orgasm. The boy asked her how long the song would take. About a minute, she replied. 'Well,' he grinned, 'I start to shake if I have to stand still for more than 30 seconds, so if you see me looking excited it's not 'cos I'm perving.'

Rolf dismisses him immediately. Great. Justice and revenge. I didn't have to say a thing, and I was right, it's been proven. Other people, though, are more difficult to deal with. It's hard to work out where I stand with them. It's still like that first day at school, trying to get into the right gang. Are they with me or not?

Mike the grip becomes slightly competitive and occasionally takes time out to tell me about how good other actors he's worked with are, and how natural their performances have been. Is he telling me this as a point of conversation, or as a way of pointing out that I am not as good? My paranoia kicks in. I can't bring myself to ask, so I avoid him where possible and smile ingratiatingly where not.

The continuity woman oscillates between flirtation and reminding me that this is the most supportive crew I will ever work with. I oscillate between flirtation and wondering if she is trying to undermine me by praising the crew. It's all far more exhausting than just doing the part.

Cameraman Ian, soundman James and first assistant director Paul all adopt a fatherly approach. Ian checks my mood each morning, James makes suggestions on how best to utilise the wig microphones for the coming scenes, Paul ensures my comfort is set up for the day and that I'm aware of what is scheduled. I lap this all up but also wonder why they would doubt me. Of course I'm okay, of course I've checked the schedules, of course I've thought through the sound options. What do they take me for?

At the same time, I'm eager to be helpful, so I keep offering suggestions about everything. They listen to my increasingly cocksure proposals with patience, and either try them out or gently explain why they will not, cannot, work. At one point, we are in the middle of a shot where I am trying to organise the placement of camera, crew and extras. It's taking a lot of time. They don't seem able to understand simple directions. Rolf wants me just to act so we can move on. He takes me aside and tells me I am becoming too focused on everybody else's area, that my performance is starting to suffer.

I am almost as hurt as I am embarrassed. Maybe he has a point, but so do I. It will be so much better my way, and then I can concentrate on acting. I want to explain, but I can't, we don't have the time. I flush with shame. Minutes later, I notice a photographer pointing his camera at me. He is the third unknown photographer to do so today, and he's not with the film, and I don't know who he is, and I'm smarting, and I yell at him: 'Why are you taking my photo? I don't even know who you are! We're trying to make a film here! If you want to take photos, then ask!'

He apologises and moves off, much to my delight. At lunch that day I learn that he is the Kodak representative who has given us so much new stock at wholesale prices. Rolf tells me that of all the days I could have thrown a wobbly this was the worst, but it's okay because the Kodak guy was very understanding. My ego is like a slippery dip.

But if the ego's a slippery dip, my ethics are up for sale. My ability to compromise surprises me. I don't know why: I'd read the script. It was clear we were going to do some pretty awful things. Somehow I'd managed not to think about them, and now as they happen I hardly raise a complaint. There is a scene in which Bubby plays with dismembered cockroaches. *Confessor Caressor* Tim has been sitting all morning quietly cutting the insects' legs off with scissors, and I am disturbed at the sight and the actuality. It's something I don't really approve of. I hover around, trying to think of ways of avoiding the scene. 'Do you think they feel the pain?' I ask primly. 'Nah,' says Tim, 'we put them in the freezer first.' This makes me feel better. When the time comes, I have no problem playing with the dismembered, slowly thawing insects until we get the shot.

The cat is harder. Bubby has a cat, which he unknowingly traumatises and then kills by accident. Our studio cat has been taken from an animal shelter's death row for feral cats. It has to be killed unless it finds a home. Our cat will be looked after for the few days it is on set, then returned to the vet and killed. We will then use the dead body.

In between times, I'm meant to make the cat hiss and spit. This isn't so hard: it spits and hisses most of the time. It's scared. It's probably spent all its life spitting and hissing. We get to a scene where the cat is tied to a chair for Bubby to shout at it. It's pretty calm about being tied up. It sits quietly all through the rehearsal. But once the camera starts, the cat goes crazy. It tries to get off the chair but can't because of the ropes. It panics. The cat is so frantic, the chair nearly falls over. I wonder if I should stop the scene, try to calm the cat down. But I also know how good this looks on camera, and I know no one can get near the animal anyway. It's too wild. So I carry on.

We have more scenes to do with the cat, but Rolf is traumatised. 'I feel like an SS man,' he says. 'We have to stop.' We all agree. We feel terrible. We can't go the extra step of putting the cat through more scenes.

So we send it to the vet.

The film continues, and so does my ethical transformation. One night we turn up to film at a restaurant. The owner has agreed to allow his poorly attended eatery in the middle of an industrial area to be used as a location. Someone has told him it will be very good for business to have us film there. He believes them. On the night, he even decides to provide the catering. Twenty extras, the crew, and most of his family and friends arrive. As we film, a pig is roasted for us, but some men turn up saying they are family, carve it up and take it away along with two bottles of whisky. The owner is distraught, and we are hungry. He suddenly has to make 40 dinners to feed us all. He makes his wife do it, and sits at the table with Rolf and me. He explains how he is going to extend the eatery, make it twice the size to fit the crowds who will come once the film is released. Rolf tries to tell him this may not happen, but he doesn't really listen. He calls his children over to perform.

We have met them before. Rolf took me here to see the place before we started filming, and we had dinner while the two children were forced to play the violin for us. We clapped after each piece, which encouraged the father to shout at his children to play more. It went on for an hour or so before the youngest, possibly ten years old, became fatigued with the weight and the pressure. We managed to get him to allow them to stop when we noticed what looked like blood on the fretboard. We had to be careful how we did it. We wanted the place as a location.

This evening he wants them to play again, but we manage to stop him. We haven't the time. He turns to me and brings his eldest child forward. 'She wants to be an actress,' he says. 'You must help her.' She blushes – she is all of 13 and very shy. It is an awkward moment. We need to keep the restaurant man happy for the film's sake.

'Okay,' I say, 'I'll help.'

She is radiant; her father smiles. The pig and whisky loss is forgotten. I have been successful. Filming won't be disrupted.

Rolf turns to me. 'You should honour that promise,' he says.

'Mmm,' I answer, miffed. I'd expected a bit more gratitude. After all, no one else is being particularly altruistic.

The film creates its own impetus, which takes over everything. A few nights later we are in a wrecker's yard with rusty tin iron and broken glass all round, racing against the sunrise, trying to complete the shot before the beginning of daylight. Beverly is hurriedly applying dirt to the three extras who are to play tramps, and Ian is measuring the extent of the encroaching morning light. The rest of us are waiting for them to finish, gathered in a group ready to start. Suddenly we hear a loud, dull thud, like a bag of concrete hitting the ground. Everyone turns, and we see someone behind us having an epileptic fit on the concrete footpath amid the rust and glass. There is a moment of stasis as we all look at him thrashing around. Then Beverly dives in and begins to clear the glass from around him, and tries to keep his movements controlled. Someone shouts, 'Get the nurse, get the nurse!' Beverly shouts back, 'It is the nurse, it is the nurse!' We all laugh. We can't help it. Someone phones an ambulance, someone sits with the nurse as his fit begins to calm down, and the first assistant director shouts, 'Okay, back to work, the sun'll be up soon.' We all turn around and go back to filming the shot of me and the tramps in the wrecker's yard as the nurse with his bruised head slowly stops spasming. The shot never gets used.

Days later, I have a scene with Rachel, a woman with cerebral palsy whose character has fallen in love with Bubby, and who learns that he is not in love with her. Yes, Rolf has managed to find a way of replacing the children with adults. He's incorporating Rachel's own personal story of unrequited love for her carer into Bubby's development of a sense of responsibility. The scene requires Rachel to be immensely upset, and for Bubby to become equally as upset. Rachel the actor has such an advanced form of cerebral palsy she finds it very difficult to translate extreme emotions into physical reactions, and it takes her a great many tries to get there. But she does.

I have difficulty with tears. Upset isn't hard, tears are. The wait hasn't helped. Neither has Rachel's ability to find her way to the emotional state that brings tears on. She is an untrained actor with extreme cerebral palsy. I'm supposed to be the professional, and the tears won't come. Mike the grip tells me he's never worked with an actor who can't cry on demand. Bastard. Now I know he thinks I'm useless, but it doesn't help the tears to come. Make-up Beverly tells me this is common; she has a way of dealing with it which she says she learnt from Jeremy Irons. Phew, someone big. Stuff Mike, obviously he hasn't worked with people like Jeremy Irons, what would he know? The method, explains Beverly, involves blowing gently into the eyes through a tube of Vicks VapoRub. The menthol creates an irritation that brings on tears. Easy.

As soon as Rachel hits the emotional mark, my eyes are held open and menthol is blown into them. There's not much time, everyone is anxious, and the menthol comes out at gale force. My right eye especially is affected – it burns so much I scream. Rolf asks if I'm okay, but he's already told me that this is our last day with Rachel. My eye feels like it is being burnt out, which it is, but we do the scene. Three times, with cutaways. Then, because we need to, because of time constraints, because we're on a roll, we do another scene where Bubby meets two groupies and dismisses them because they're not Angel, the girl he is in love with. I can hardly see the actors playing the groupies, my eyes are virtually losing their vision. We do that scene a couple of times, too, then I insist on seeing a doctor. I'm going blind, I can't see where I'm going, I can't do another scene. I am ridden with guilt.

It turns out the menthol has burnt the top layer of the epithelium from my cornea, and I need to cover it for 24 hours to allow it to grow back. I am so affected by the impetus of the film that I suggest shooting the next few scenes all in profile so that the bandage won't show, but Rolf disagrees. 'We can use the insurance,' he says. 'We'll shoot for an extra day. We can't have you damaged.'

Beverly insists that I just have weak eyes. I let it go. I'm not interested in apportioning blame. I'm thinking that I worked in the staff-pay section of the post office for five years. By the time I left, I'd used up all my sick leave and was well into borrowing from the next year's – anything not to have to go to work. I was up to eight toilet breaks a day just to get out of the office and sit alone in the cubicle. Imagine that. The toilet cubicle was a better option than the office. It says a lot, one way or another.

But here, I struggle on through severe pain. I wait several hours with the outer layer of my cornea burning away so we can complete two scenes. I offer to continue working while the cornea tries to rebuild itself. What is the motivation? Do I really think the film will not be completed if I tend to my eye? Do I really think my vision is less important than the film?

Yes, I do. I am totally bemused.

And I'm joyous. My own life disappears into the making of the film. Do you have any idea how great that can feel? For 11 weeks I lose all sense of responsibility to the outside world or my place in it. I don't see anyone, I don't cook, I don't go out, and I don't notice. That area of life is put into suspended animation.

It reaches a peak on the two nights we use to film the band gig scenes. I sleep during the day, then go to work at night. There are about 40 or 50 extras who will be the audience for the band. On the second night, when we film a major concert scene in which the audience is aping Bubby, Rolf gets just slightly drunk. He's in his element directing the crowd. He has very few suggestions on how I should play it – he's more concerned with them. I improvise, pooling movements and actions from various characters in the film and performing them in front of the audience. They react. I know they're paid to, but I love it. It's frenzied, a fantasy melding of actor meets rock star meets wild child. When we finish, the sun is coming up and the day is beginning. I go home to sleep.

I feel like I have entered a world of outlandish hours, where I am the star of a circus that exists to highlight me, the evidence appearing magically 24 hours later when we watch rushes in the cinema of the Film Corporation. My image magnified beyond belief. I know it's a child's world but I'm totally in awe, at once overly excited yet painfully aware that this me-centred universe could disappear at any moment. I develop a series of routines and habits before each shot, crawling down the street like a cat to get into character before the take, then burping uncontrollably up until the word 'Action!'. I find myself unable to perform without the ritual. It is as if at these junctures all reality disappears, the world is dispelled by entering the fantasy, and an instant of ecstasy occurs in which responsibility doesn't exist except in terms of finding the moment and coinciding it with the camera and the placement and the music in my head. And when it works, the feeling of achievement and release is an addictive rush. Everybody around me accepts my need to do this, and waits silently until I'm finished. I have licence, even respect, to be a complete idiot. I am totally hooked.

Eleven weeks after we begin, we stop.

CHAPTER 2
the first taste

Whyalla, 1966

Nineteen sixty-six. Ten-pounds assisted passage to come to an Australia desperate for European tradesmen. *The Australis* was part of the Chandris Line, a Greek shipping company. The trip from Portsmouth had taken four weeks, a record speed for a passenger liner. I'd been sick for most of it, missing the illegal migrants who came on in Aden, Yemen. Everyone said they were Greek even though that didn't make sense, but they had the same olive skin as the Greek crew so they must have been. They slept on the decks, taught everyone who wasn't sick how to enjoy the Greek food, got the normally reserved Anglos to play volleyball and table tennis. My sister and brothers were out there all the time. I wanted to join in, too, I could see the illegals from my bed if I looked out of the porthole, but I never got to meet them. They were imprisoned in Fremantle, to the mixed response of the northern English ten-pounders who had befriended them on the voyage. The captain of *The Australis* committed suicide shortly after.

I slept on the floor of the train carriage from Melbourne to Port Adelaide and only just started to recover on the bus trip from Adelaide on. It was interminable, frightening. After Port Augusta, with its ramshackle houses, tin roofs and colonial cowboy architecture, one of the adults told a joke. 'A Muslim man came to Australia,' he began in a broad Mancunian accent, 'and got on this bus. When they let him off, he fell to his knees and cried, "Why, Allah, Why?" And that's how they named the town!'

The adults round me laughed uneasily. I wondered why. I wasn't laughing. I was looking out the window. It was the end of the six-year drought, there were dead sheep and cows and kangaroos littered by the sides of the roads, and desert as far as the eye could see, and if we'd driven this long in the UK we'd surely have covered the country twice over. Maybe it wasn't such a joke. Maybe that *was* why the place was called Whyalla. Maybe those photographs we'd been shown by the suited, smarmy, gentle press gang of the immigration department – green botanic gardens, tended footpaths, full, pleasingly appointed shopping centres – *were* from some-where else, like my teacher had said. Even at six years of age I knew this wasn't funny. I knew it was fake laughter.

Everyone went silent as the bus drove past the steelworks and the rusting, battered sign that read: 'WHYALLA. POP. 22,000'. Nobody spoke as we drove past a few desultory shops, then down a long, deserted road, then stopped at the corrugated-iron hangars of the Milpara Migrant Hostel. No one moved as we looked in bewilderment at what appeared to be a jail, until one brave woman asked loudly, 'Where's the town?'

'We just drove through it, love,' answered the driver.

'It's a hell on earth,' said Dad a few days later. Mum, I could tell, didn't know whether to laugh or cry, she had that expression that could go either way. We were all standing in the Housing Trust house that wasn't yet finished, shaking to blasts of dynamite. Mount Laura, the small hill breaking the flatness of the landscape beyond the kitchen window, was being excavated every Sunday to create shale for the roads, the driveways and the footpaths of all the new migrant suburbs. Soon, I thought, there'd be no Mount Laura left to break the flatness. The houses would stop, and then there'd be the desert until your eyes stopped seeing. Desert and dust.

Red dust. Rust red. Can you see it? I can. Pumping out of the coke ovens of the BHP steelworks at night, or blowing in from the cleared scrub when the winds turned. So fine it stung, blasting us bare-legged children and our overburdened mothers walking home from the far-flung shops, so that we cried with pain, sometimes bled. Hiding the rows and rows and rows of low-level, semi-detached Housing Trust migrant houses, and burying the stunted attempts at European gardens in yet another layer of oxide and grit. Settling on the washing hung out on the Hills hoist washing lines, getting into the cooking and the glasses and the fridge, and covering the framed photographs from home – those reminders of greenery and clouds and robins and worms and populated streets. No more, said the dust, no more.

When the dust was sleeping, the sun had its turn. Harsher than a spotlight, and constant. Inching through a sky bigger than any we migrants had seen. Roads becoming sticky with heat, little mirages of water magically appearing in the distance – nature's cruel joke about bitumen. Migrant houses boiling beneath corrugated-iron roofs squealing with expansion. Bricks, concrete, cars, shoes – all suddenly too hot to touch. Good husbands, good fathers braved the heat and the sun to hose down the houses in the middle of the day. There was so much perspiration, chemists dispensed salt tablets that made people vomit.

So you would have sworn the town was empty. The streets were, most of the time. They were wide, wide and empty. They were waiting for the rest of Europe to arrive and it hadn't. If you walked down them, there was usually only the sad, drawn-out 'aaaahhhhh' of the crows flying lazily above. There were cars sometimes, and a single bus that went round the place every hour or so. And there were the Scots, but you avoided them. If you could.

Many of the migrants came from the poorer sections of Glasgow. They were violent, dressed in denim, and travelled in packs. It wasn't a good idea to get on their bad side. Not being Scottish was one way to achieve this. So was being Scottish. They were famous for being able to deliver head-butts from a distance, and for continuing to put the boot in when you were down. They hung around the migrant areas of town, the undeveloped western side, which of course was where all the Housing Trust houses were built.

They were mad bastards and hard to avoid. You either had to fight good or run fast, and running was the better option because no matter how well you fought, they were in a pack and you were on your own.

There was this one particular day I'd been chased and caught. I'd given up, run so far I couldn't run any more. There were at least seven of them.

'It's no' him!' said the leader.

'Are ye no' Micky Martyn?' asked another.

'No,' I answered. I didn't know if this was good or bad.

'Ye look like Micky Martyn, ken, but that bastard's blond! We dinnae like Micky Martyn. Do ye?' they asked.

'I don't know him,' I lied. I went to school with Micky Martyn. He looked nothing like me. Maybe it was a trick question.

'Shall we go him enyway?' asked one.

'No,' said the leader. 'I cannae be bothered.'

I thanked them. I was so grateful, I thanked them. I can see it still, Our Lady Help of Christians school in the background, me standing on the wasteland red-dust roundabout in the middle of the road with the cars going past, thanking the mad bastards for not beating me up. Bloody hell.

There was a beach where the tide went out five miles. You could go crabbing if you liked, which I didn't, I felt sorry for the crabs. But you had to be careful. If you were out there when the tide came in, you could get caught and drown. It came in that fast. Like a nightmare.

The Lido, summer 1993

The foyer of the Hotel Des Bains is lush and busy. Rolf and I are at a loss. Our rooms won't be ready for another two hours, and jet lag is setting in. My backpack is in the corner, put there by a disapproving bellboy, but I'm holding on to the suit. I've borrowed it from the State Theatre Company of South Australia. It was made for Hugo Weaving, it's one size too big for me, and it makes me look a bit like a tramp, but I'm told I will need it to attend screenings. I'm concerned about losing it.

As we stand wondering what to do, someone famous sweeps down the spiral staircase. We aren't sure who, but we get pushed aside by a horde of paparazzi jostling for photograph opportunities. Two tourists nearby try to take their own shots but can't get past the professionals. They turn to us. 'Excuse me,' one of them asks politely, 'are you famous?'

'Do we look famous?' replies Rolf.

They take our photos anyway, just in case.

Why are we here? *Bad Boy Bubby* has been accepted into the competition section of the 1993 Venice Film Festival! It's been seven months since we finished filming it. A whole other nightmare. After 11 weeks of filming, I kept visiting the edit rooms of the film, watching it being put together. I didn't know how to let it go. I remembered how annoyed I was when Claire, my screen mother, did the same, turning up on set after her role was finished. I remembered feeling scornful at her inability to move on. I tried to convince myself that it was different for me, it was more or less my film, I *should* keep going in to check the edit, how else was I going to learn? It was quite depressing.

I even dropped into the restaurant. It'd been extended. I was the only person in the huge space. The owner complained, 'None of the film people come here. You are the first.' He brought his children out. Would I like to hear the violin? Would I like a meal? 'No, I'm just passing, I have an appointment,' I lied. I asked the eldest if she still wanted to act. She shrugged. I felt the same.

Around the same time, I'd heard that the film was having trouble finding distributors. Because of the cat. Distributors and buyers found it offensive to have such treatment screened. I had a conversation with first assistant director Paul about it. 'They aren't concerned with your being raped in the film,' Paul said, 'or any of the abuse to you. Just with the cat. They're so hypocritical.'

'Well, I wasn't really being raped or abused,' I replied. 'I was acting. The cat wasn't.'

He shook his head in bewilderment. 'Yeah . . .' he said, 'but still . . .'

The conversation had irritated me. Why hadn't anyone thought about this when we were filming? Why did they use a real cat? Why did they keep it in the edit? God knows, I was just doing my job at the time, it had nothing to do with me, and now they were ruining my only chance at being seen on screen. *What were they thinking?*

But now I can be more forgiving. True, I'm unsure what the festival is like. The only festivals I have heard of are Cannes, which I've seen on TV, and the South Australian

Adelaide Film Festival, which shows subtitled films for two weeks each year. Venice must be somewhere between the two. Besides, I backpacked here before *Bubby*, and I remember how beautiful the city is. If I can get paid to relive the film and stay in Venice at the same time, I'm not going to say no. The Australian Film Commission has given me a travel grant to cover the fare and food expenses. I've flown via London because it's cheaper than flying direct. But it also takes longer. And it's a lot more exhausting. I could hug the porter who finally tells us our rooms are ready.

There's an olde-worlde opulence to the room. Polished, aged wood, windows looking out on to a tabled verandah, a massive bouquet of flowers from the festival director, a brass bed, and a TV with a welcome message on it. It's my first time in such a room. It might be my first time in an actual hotel room, I can't remember, but nothing I've been in looked like this. I take a photo of myself beside the flowers. I test the bed. It's spongy and sags in the middle. I'll have to put the mattress on the floor to sleep. I wonder if all the rooms are like that, or just the ones for people who aren't paying.

The telephone rings. It's Rolf. His mattress is spongy too, and his cupboard door is blocked by the brass bed, which is bolted to the floor. Neither of us considers asking for a different room; we already feel like interlopers. The hotel clerk wouldn't even look at us when he was booking us in. Perhaps we're a bit out of our class.

I don't want to appear brash or ungrateful, so we agree to remain silent and go to meet our Italian producer,

Domenico, and Simona, our Venice publicist. We have a publicist! This is bigger than I thought.

Everything seems very casual. We're told we have tickets to a couple of films in the evening, we can eat afterwards, and there are a few interviews tomorrow morning before the first press screening. It's like a holiday. Giorgio, the Australian producer from Sydney, who I've never met before, has arrived. So has soundman James. We go to lunch. Giorgio pays. Phew.

By nightfall I'm in a state of hyper-exhaustion. Excitement, lack of sleep, jet lag. Domenico gets us into an Italian film that is showing in competition. I go because Rolf goes, because I don't want to insult Domenico, because I don't want to miss anything, but everything is going blurry. The whole of the festival seems to have stormed the cinema. We end up standing jammed in a crowd at the back of the screening, and the film is laborious and long, though I doze through most of it and can't distinguish between film and dream so can't really tell. The audience is very excited, and I should be able by now to understand that this event is huge, but my brain has stopped computing those things. People interact with the figures on the screen, shouting comments and laughing and moving all the time. It's annoying.

I'm completely dazed when Domenico finds me in the foyer and introduces me to Italian actress Francesca Neri. She is beautiful and surrounded by autograph hunters. Something about the associated glamour wakes me up. We gather Rolf and James and his wife, and wander off to have dinner. It is late, and the open-air restaurant that Francesca wants has just closed. The manager approaches to turn us away but recognises Francesca immediately and reopens the restaurant. Photographers surround her, calling out her name. '*Compassione*,' she murmurs quietly, holding her hands up butterfly-style. She allows them a couple of minutes before waving lightly to signify the end. Restaurant staff shoo the photographers away. I am in awe.

Breakfast the next morning is free. There is a huge range of foods available to us, and I stuff myself with a three-course meal before making large sandwiches for my lunch. The AFC grant doesn't quite cover the expense of eating on the Lido, the island off the main city of Venice where the festival is held, and I'm not sure how far I can expect Domenico's generosity to go. The hotel staff look disparaging, as normal, and I feel rebellious. I'm getting more out of them than they planned on giving. It's revenge for the saggy mattress.

The Hotel Des Bains is a one-kilometre walk from the Hotel Excelsior, where most of the interviews take place. There is a shuttle bus between the two hotels every half hour, with a stop for the main cinema where the competition screenings are held. There are also ferries operated by the Hotel Excelsior which go to the mainland. They too are free. All you have to do is show your room card, and over you go. It's how life should be. I could get used to this.

Rolf and I walk along the Lido's beach to the Excelsior for the morning's interviews. We sit in the middle of the plaza. The day is glorious. I look around at all the beautiful people. There is a constant parade of elegant, fashion-conscious women walking their dogs up and down the beach. Those who have paid for the privilege lounge in deck-chairs on the sand, while all around us actors and directors I don't recognise conduct interviews with the press.

I want to be part of this world.

The journalists who interview us don't seem very interested. They ask about the state of the Australian film industry. They talk to Rolf about the reality of using 32 directors of photography. They ask if we have seen any Italian films and what we think of them. They don't seem to have seen our film, or if they have they don't mention it. I'm disheartened and Simona is impatient. The press screening will take place today, the competition screening tomorrow. She needs more interviews and photo sessions, but it's difficult when nothing about the film is known. She can't get any good journalists interested.

So I was right. They *haven't* seen it.

Rolf is concerned about other things. He is waiting for his US agent to arrive and is wondering how the sleeping arrangements will work. Marty is paying for his trip himself and hasn't the funds for a hotel. He and Rolf will share a bed. Rolf seems fairly relaxed about this, he's just unsure how the hotel will react. Marty, he explains, isn't a typical LA agent.

When Marty arrives, I can see what Rolf means. I haven't met an LA agent, but Marty's hair and beard are long and straggly. He is dressed in a baggy T-shirt, baggy jeans, desert boots. He's self-obsessed, loud, concerned that sleeping in the same bed as Rolf may give people the wrong idea. He isn't what I imagined an LA agent to be.

That night I get in free to watch the competition screening of Robert Altman's *Short Cuts*. That huge screen full of American stars and the rapturous audience response depresses the hell out of me. I can't imagine ever getting there. And I'd like to. This is a pretty good life. I wouldn't mind it all the time.

I meet up with Rolf, Domenico, James and Simona afterwards, and Simona reports that the press screenings went 'reasonably well'. No one left, no one booed. I'm not impressed. At *Short Cuts*, everyone cheered.

We all go to dinner with Maria and Lucia, the sales agents from Intra Films who are dealing with *Bad Boy Bubby*. They both look, act and dress like models. Marty thinks I may stand a chance with Lucia because I'm the star of the film. He tells me I should put the word on her. I tell him it's not likely, I'm a nerdy Catholic from an all-boys' school, I'm incapable of putting the word on anyone. He shrugs and rides off on the bicycle he has rented to do a tour of the Lido. It's two a.m.

The next morning I meet Rolf for breakfast. I eat my three-course meal and prepare my sandwiches while Rolf explains why he is so tired. Marty got lost on his bicycle, nearly had an accident, didn't get back until late. Slept in his clothes and boots. No chance of anyone getting the wrong impression there. The bed sagged even more with both of them in it, there was no room to put the mattress on the floor because of the suitcases, and the cupboard couldn't be opened because of the bed . . . I think about offering him my room but don't. I laugh. It has just struck me what a good time I'm having. I haven't had to pay for anything yet, I'm in the hotel that was the location for *Death In Venice*, Rolf has a crazily unconventional American agent sharing his bed, and I'm hanging around with famous people I don't recognise but who keep getting asked for photos and autographs. It's so bizarre. I stuff my sandwiches in my bag. It's time to go to the press conference. The press conference! Me!

We meet the others along the way and walk towards the Excelsior. I'm not sure what to expect. As we get closer we can see that the doors are blocked by a large crowd. I remember that someone said Harrison Ford was arriving today, and I think how typical it is that he should arrive just as we are about to have a press conference. Simona is unconcerned. She explains that the conference is of little importance, just a formality, the important stuff happens afterwards with individual interviews. I start to forgive Harrison. I even think of him like that. Harrison. Just another actor doing a press conference about a lead role in a film. Like me. Nicholas.

The crowd literally have their backs to us as they jostle to get in. Rolf and I both have broad-brimmed hats on for sun protection, and our faces are shadowed. Simona and Domenico start to push a way through for us, shouting something in Italian. I assume they're explaining we have a conference to attend. The crowd judders a little and I decide

41

Harrison must be in view. But then people start to turn and look. Someone shouts, 'Bad Boy Bubby!' with a heavy Italian accent. People start taking photos. Rolf laughs. Someone thrusts out a piece of paper and a pen. People start yelling at us. Then the clapping starts.

It hits me with a shock: they're here for us!

We are late getting into the conference room because it's hard for me to say no to the autographs. I'd do it all day. When we do arrive, the room is full.

I can hardly hear the questions I am so excited. Someone compares me to Jack Nicholson in *The Shining*. Everyone claps. I make some quip about not getting paid as much. They clap again. Rolf answers questions slowly and with thought. I fire off whatever comes into my head in an attempt to sound intelligent. It doesn't matter. They love us. I love them.

We are taken from the conference room to a podium outside, which has the festival's insignia hung behind it. It's surrounded by photographers, 100 or more so far as I can guess. I am totally unprepared for this. Rolf and I step on to the podium, and the photographers start. They are all shouting, 'Mr Rolf, Mr Nick, here, here! Please Mr Nick! Bubby Bubby Bubby! Mr de Heer!'

We spend a couple of seconds in shocked non-coordination, though both of us immediately take on victory smiles. It's instinctive. Then we work out a sweeping motion with our heads, to allow everyone to get a face-on photo of us both. We do a lot of sweeps. I am ecstatic.

The film has become a hot favourite overnight, and now

the press are lining up to speak to us. I am a little worried. I'm not sure what it is they are reacting to. I haven't seen the finished film yet. But I don't let that stop me.

Simona has a list of people for us to talk to. She has only allowed a few interviews today as the competition screening is in a few hours, but tomorrow will be full. Already journalists are starting to follow us with long-lens photographers in tow, and already Simona is heading them off. I can't for the life of me understand why. I'm ready to talk to anyone. I keep posing for photographs while the others gently nudge me on. It strikes me how pretty a lot of the female journalists are. I'm surprised I hadn't noticed before.

James, who grew up in the same town as me, is grinning widely as he watches me with the photographers, and watches how the journalists cluster round. He takes my arm as we walk back to the hotel to prepare for the competition screening. 'Look around, Nicky,' he says. 'It's a long way from Whyalla, isn't it?'

He's right. This is as far from Whyalla as you could hope to get. It's inconceivable, a dream come true – except back there standing on that Whyalla beach looking at the water five miles away, this dream never even occurred. I float to the foyer of the Excelsior in my oversize Hugo Weaving suit, along the beach promenade where the tide *never* goes out. When I get there it's buzzing. There are a lot of women in air-hostess costumes, attempting to manage the crowd. The festival is sponsored by an airline, and the security/publicity staff are wearing the airline uniforms as advertising. Domenico is deep in conversation with Francesca. People are nudging and pointing at Rolf and me. Masses of them seem to join our group and are greeted by Maria and Lucia. Marty turns up in the same jeans and T-shirt, with a dinner jacket thrown over the top. Giorgio and his wife introduce me to a series of men and women whose names I instantly forget. I practise my one line of Italian: '*Scusi, ma non parli Italiano, sono Inglese*,' and they laugh. It seems I have learnt from a Sicilian. Then, suddenly, we are moving.

There is a red carpet all the way from the foyer of the Excelsior to the main competition cinema. In front of us is a motorised platform with TV spotlights playing over us, and TV cameras filming our procession. Other cameras dart around us. People crowd the street to watch us, waving and clapping. They haven't even seen the film yet. Flashes go off, and the air hostesses act as security guards. It's almost too much, I am starting to feel embarrassed. What if the film's not any good? What if all this sudden hype backfires? What if I sit there and hate my performance?

We get to the cinema, we are introduced to festival director Gino Pontecorvo, we are led to our seats. They are spotlit, directly in the middle of the auditorium. There is nowhere to hide, no way of getting out unnoticed. I look around. In the midst of the excitement, I am disappointed. The cinema is about three-quarters full. *Short Cuts* was packed and the Italian film was overflowing.

And then I see myself.

The screen is huge, and the opening shot is a close-up of my face being shaved. In the script, the opening was a montage of the room, so this takes me by surprise. It's kind of confronting. I am 20 or 30 times the size of life up there. I have to decide what I think. It's good. I *like* myself with hair, and Beverly's wig makes my eyes shine so. I *really* like being that *big*. In fact, I'm mesmerised by my image. This must be how Narcissus felt. I could sit here all night.

The screening becomes a blur. Once that first moment is over, I break out in a cold sweat. Rolf has sunk down in his chair in an attempt to become invisible. Marty is whooping and laughing at the end of our row. Domenico is as cool as ever. When the cat scenes occur, a section of the audience stands up and makes as if to leave, arguing loudly with those around them, and then sits back down. The audience goes from being noisy to being very silent. I worry about a band scene where the sound editors have wrecked a clever bit of timing and made me look bad. I worry that the ending is too schmaltzy. When the credits begin to roll, there is a longish pause. I just want to leave.

And then they start standing and clapping and turning round to us, and the lights flash on and they start shouting. I don't totally understand, it's like a fantasy, we don't know what to do. We stand and raise our hands, and bow, and sit, and they continue. We do it again, and they go wilder. It just keeps going. 'I think they're genuine,' I say to Rolf, and he replies, 'I think you may be right.' Domenico turns to me and says, 'Go! Go!', so I push my way out, being congratulated and touched all the way. I wait outside for a minute or so, and Domenico comes running out and drags me back in. 'I meant go to them,' he explains. 'It is the tradition.' They are still on their feet and cheering, and I want so much to go down among them, but I can't, not yet. I love this, but it is just a film and the promised adulation is beyond my ability to accept. It's like the first time sex was a possibility: I could've cried with relief but there was so much expectation I just couldn't go through with it. We all raise our arms again and then leave as a group before the clapping stops. I feel drugged.

The first public screening occurs immediately afterwards in an adjacent cinema holding more than 1000 people, and word is out so the cinema is completely full. Domenico tells me it's my job to be presented along with Rolf at the end of the screening. This time I am prepared. The cheering starts as the credits role, and the whole crowd leaps up when we are presented. I go in front of the screen, hold my arms out wide, take in the entire audience for an ecstatic, glorious 30 seconds, then bow. The crowd loves it. So do I. A woman in a wheelchair throws a flower and I hold it up to the crowd, then drag the reluctant Rolf and Domenico forwards. It is my showman moment. I have never felt so confident or ebullient or capable. I salute the audience again. People start shouting and throwing programs and stamping their feet. I lead the way out. I can tell we could stay longer, the clapping and cheering aren't about to ebb, but I can tell, too, that there is a dignity in choosing the moment to leave, and I've judged it right. The others wouldn't have known. I am in charge. It is my film, my moment, my audience.

Rolf just grins.

The world has never looked so beautiful.

Life on the Lido changes overnight. We are besieged by journalists, photographers, well-wishers and autograph hunters. Simona has people queuing up to interview us, and she picks and chooses carefully. I have three full days of photograph shoots, starting at nine a.m. and rolling through until four p.m., with interviews slotted in between. We sit in the Excelsior plaza and become one of a series of directors and actors being interviewed, but for us the television crews wait patiently in line. I oscillate between my own version of charm for the print journalists, and feral, angsty posturing for the cameras of the glossy magazines. I recognise with glee the effect it has to be polite and courteous to journalists whose looks I like, when they expect someone wild and Bubbyish; and I love the excitement that photographers exhibit as I prostitute myself, clawing cat-like at mirrors or leaping demonically into the air against the background of the Lido Beach. I learn what answers get the correct responses and how best to deliver them as if it is the first time they are given. It's fantastic. Everyone adores the film. Everyone adores the fact that I am not the character. It's so odd, so easy, so wonderful to understand the simple trick of interviews. They've been talking to actors for years, and they're still surprised that actors can act. I can't go wrong.

The fantasy of fame starts to take over. A French TV presenter straddles me during one interview, and whisperingly asks if I have a girlfriend. I hesitate. I'm not sure if

I can handle where this might go and, after all, they're filming it. 'I do,' I reply, 'in Australia.'

'That,' she whispers in my ear, 'is a long way away.' I am seduced. I wish I'd said no. I'm suddenly ready to believe she was asking me seriously. After all, I have to admit I've become an overnight star. These things happen, why deny it? 'I hope you make it,' she says afterwards. 'You're sweet.' I'm not sure I *want* to be sweet.

Rolf and I meet for coffee in between interviews, only to be surrounded by long-lens cameras, microphones to catch what we might say, and simple requests for autographs. We don't get to talk, but that's okay. Later in the day, a young girl runs over to where we are sitting and thrusts a wad of photos in my hand. They are of her, skimpily dressed in various poses, with her phone number on the back. She thinks we can get her into film. I play with the thought of sexual bribery but dismiss it. I'm not that far gone yet, but I am enjoying this. I take time out to walk alone on the beach and exult inwardly when I see three camera crews follow me. I wander coyly around, pretending I haven't noticed them.

The walk between the two hotels becomes a parade of fame. I get old women approaching me to shake my hand, young men and women taking their tops off to have their bodies signed, offers of sex, phone numbers thrust into my hands, gifts. I make excuses to keep doing the walk. One night I wander into a nightclub with Marty and get virtually kidnapped by a gang of youths who become violently proprietorial about my presence there. Marty saves me in a show of uncharacteristic altruism. People buy me drinks, want to be my friend, point me out on the street. On a ferry to the mainland one night all the passengers give me a standing ovation. I continue with increasingly strange photo shoots and interviews, finally pausing early one morning to enquire about the relevance of my holding an unknown baby in one hand and a surfboard in the other. 'Bubby Aussie,' explains the journalist, but this one I can't bring myself to do.

A day or so later we are sitting at a pavement café as Marty explains in increasing frustration just how he wants his French fries done. The Italian waiter looks contemptuous as Marty's voice raises: 'Don't you understand, I want them soft in the middle, browned on the edges, and not too thick!' Rolf leans over: 'Marty, this is Italy, not America. They're just chips here.' At that moment, we hear from a distance the familiar cries of 'Bubby! Bubby! Bubby!'. We all turn to look, wondering where the onslaught will appear from. A larger than usual crowd of paparazzi is surging down the street, surrounding another crowd of ten or so bodyguards, themselves surrounding a short man who is ignoring the shouting. Now the words become clearer: 'Bobby! Bobby! Bobby!'

Robert De Niro is in town.

It is the beginning of the end. Spielberg arrives around the same time to launch *Jurassic Park*. I walk past the steps of his hotel as the same photographers who've been following me into cafés and bars push me out of the way to get a better view of the entrance. Harvey Keitel runs around the streets with his head down, pulling a wave of journalists in his wake. John Turturro throws a tantrum at breakfast, shouting at the waiting paparazzi to leave him alone. They don't. I smile at them, signalling my willingness to be photographed. They smile back but don't snap. I, too, want to have a tantrum. I want to hit the table, I want to shout out to everybody, 'They said I was as good as Jack Nicholson in *The Shining*!' My cheeks are burning and my hands start to shake as I butter my lunchtime sandwich. Rolf notices, leans over and whispers, 'Is it really what you want?' I don't have the answer.

In the afternoon Rolf and I make a trip together to the mainland. I want him to experience Venice as I did when I first came. We wander through the streets and over the bridges, and he makes notes for a developing script. We sit in a square to drink coffee, and one person comes up to congratulate me on the film. I introduce him to Rolf. The man shakes our hands and leaves. Rolf softly points out how impossible this event is for the Robert De Niros of the world. Bubby can walk freely around Venice. Bobby needs ten bodyguards. 'You could be on the edge of going that way,' he says. 'Be sure what it is you want.'

It is the day before the awards are announced, but Domenico and, it seems, the whole of the Lido already know the results. We have won the special jury prize; we have also won the *Ciak* (popular) prize for best film and best actor, shared with Harvey Keitel, and the critics' prize, shared with *Short Cuts*, and the Catholic jury bronze prize. We haven't won the prize everyone said we would win: the best actor award. I try not to show my utter, gut-wrenching dis-appointment. 'That's great,' I say. Domenico tells me that there was a trade-off. The jury needed to award an Italian prize because this was an Italian festival, so the best actor award went to an Italian actor. I am not sure if he's just trying to make me feel better. I smile bravely. 'Anyway,' he says, 'the jury prize is better for the film.'

The award ceremony is held in the Piazza San Marco and is televised. We have to go a couple of hours early – something to do with the television arrangements – but the first hour or so is taken up with a special on *Jurassic Park*. I get to sit behind Gong Li, China's most famous actress. I consider touching her on the shoulder to tell her how much I admire her acting, but I'll be damned if I can remember the names of any of her films. Maybe she's seen my film, I think, maybe she'll turn around, recognise me, and tell *me* how much she enjoyed *my* acting. I can see she's not watching the *Jurassic Park* special, but she doesn't turn around. I lean forward. I need to see her profile again, it's so perfect. She's reading a book, in Chinese.

Rolf is next to one of Robert De Niro's bodyguards. Great. De Niro's bodyguards get the front row. Me, I'm hidden several rows back, the trade-off, swamped in my too-big suit made for someone else. It's ironic but I'm not smirking. Looking around, I can see director Roman Polanski in the front row, and his wife several rows behind. He keeps getting up to run back and canoodle with her. Flashbulbs go off every time this happens. My status can't be that bad if Polanski's wife is further back than me.

I should just let it go, there's nothing I can do about it. But I can see the Italian best actor sitting up there in row number one with all the other prize winners, and Domenico's story is in my head and if I were that actor surely I'd refuse to accept the award . . .

The *Jurassic Park* special goes on and on and on.

The jury, headed by Peter Weir, finally arrive. Someone sent them off to a restaurant while the *Jurassic Park* thing was on but forgot to send the gondolier back for them. They decided to get one themselves, but the festival security wouldn't let a non-official gondolier through. They've had to send a messenger to get an official to verify that they are indeed the jury. It's very late.

The ceremony is chaotic. Each winner or presenter is sent off afterwards to be photographed behind a curtain to the side of the stage, as the next prize is announced by the next celebrity presenter. People keep bumping into each other on their way back and forth. But it's functioning, until De Niro goes backstage to the waiting paparazzi. Their shouts drown out the next presentation. Out in the audience, one photographer gets forcibly removed by De Niro's bodyguards during someone else's speech. It's hard to know what to concentrate on. I'm almost enjoying it. People look a little scared up there on the stage, as if they don't know what's going on. And they don't. Our special jury prize is presented by Peter Weir, but he hasn't been told which prize he's presenting. There is a translator on stage who whispers in his ear, but he can't quite make out her accent, and he just hears the word 'Lyon', and assumes that as head of the jury he is presenting the first prize for best film, the Golden Lion. This year, that prize is shared between *Short Cuts* and *Three Colours Blue*, so he makes a speech about the difficulty of choosing between two films, and how the jury couldn't decide which was the more deserving. Then he turns to present the award.

Rolf has asked me to come on stage with him, so at least there are two of us there, but Weir blushes then blanches when he sees us both. It's a major mistake – he hasn't said a word about our film, and he's just given away which films have won the Golden Lion to an audience that now looks very puzzled. Have we won it? Or are we invading the stage in protest? Or has the chairman of the jury completely stuffed it? Obviously the latter. Weir leaves the stage and, as he later tells us, stays in his hotel room for the rest of the night, too embarrassed to come out. But we haven't noticed. It's too exciting for Rolf, and I can't decide what I think or feel. I just want to be linked in public with this bloody award. Rolf lets me hold it while he gives a victory speech. When he finishes, I try to shout a 'thank you' to the crowd. I want my moment. But the translator has stepped in, my shout is lost, I just look like a wannabe in a suit that's too big for me. I can feel the chance of fame slipping away, but no, I mustn't, I can't, I won't let it . . .

There is a party arranged for the winners after the ceremony. Nobody is sure how to get there, but there's a rumour there are gondoliers and ferries to transport us. Rolf and I are pushed along with the crowd and, after a lot of struggling, manage to get on the last boat. I'm very excited.

This, I realise, is my last chance to play up as a star, to accept the glory, indulge in a promised seduction, schmooze with overseas directors, grab that chance, and get terribly drunk for free. I want to exorcise the thwarted expectation of best actor.

When the boat arrives at the dock we can see the crowd milling into the most exquisite building, and there is a teasing view of candlelit chandeliers and frescoed walls. We are about to join them when we hear our names being called. Marty is standing in a water taxi speeding towards our ferry, his lanky hair streaming behind him in the wind, a bad hair commercial. He's been sent by Domenico and Maria to find us. They are having a dinner in our honour, we must be there. And Marty hasn't any money to pay the taxi, it's really expensive, so we have to go or at least lend him some dosh. Rolf tells me I can choose, but he must go.

I am thwarted. I would feel guilty to let him go alone. How could I face him if I did? And what if Domenico took umbrage? He's an important producer. What should I do?

By the time we arrive they have eaten. The party is only partly for us. It is also in honour of the man who got the best actor award. He is a friend of Domenico, and Maria, and Lucia. I can't see any spare chairs around, but three are found for us and we are sequestered off at the end of the table. The best actor is at the head, with his fuck-off award, and he's surrounded by people congratulating him, and he's laughing and smiling. I am furious. I take my spoon and inadvertently bend it into a half moon. Rolf sees it. 'You should keep that,' he says, 'as a reminder.' Yeah, I think, bent spoon, how wild.

Marty and I decide we can't stomach this any more, all these self-satisfied people gloating over some stupid prize. They should go get a life! We decide to get back to the big party, and somehow we cadge a ride from a private boat, but by the time we get there the whole thing is finished. I stand under the majestic chandeliers, surrounded by frescoed walls, watching the staff pack up. Everyone has left. The room is empty. The party is over. I have been cheated.

The next day as we prepare to leave, we find that there is a problem with the hotel bill. We've been eating the wrong breakfast and have amassed a $40 charge each day. There are no signs to indicate that there is a distinction in the breakfasts available, but that doesn't matter. We've also been charged for the ferries to and from the airport, and to and from the mainland. None of it was free. I feel sick.

Domenico looks after it. Rolf and I stand behind him, ignored. Our bluff has been called, we're back to the first day again. The staff don't see us.

The Lido has emptied, all the beautiful people have gone back to Rome. We get a taxi to the airport and Domenico pays for it while I say goodbye to Rolf. He and Domenico are also going to Rome, to work on the new script that Domenico is financing, and that I'm not in. I go back to Adelaide, the long way round, the cheaper flight. I arrive back just in time to sign on for unemployment benefits.

Sydney, summer 1993

What now? There's a world out there of stardom and respect and promise, and I've had a taste of it. It was so near and so tantalising, regardless of what Rolf said, yet somehow it's just fizzled out. No one in Adelaide even knows there was a film made here. It doesn't look like any more will be, either. The sun is still baking the asphalt, the streets are still empty, the State Theatre Company is still bringing its actors in from Sydney and Melbourne. What I should do, of course, is move.

Marty has taken to ringing and begging me to come to the States. He tells me he'll represent me, that I should come now while the film still lives in people's minds. He sends me a copy of the film-industry magazine *Variety*, with a huge one-page advert he's taken out congratulating his clients Rolf de Heer and Nicholas Hope on their success in Venice, which lists and quotes the reviews. It's pretty amazing. A lot of critics from around the world say very nice things about me. 'Now's the time,' says Marty. 'Come on over.'

It's tempting. But the part of me that worked in the post office for five years is scared of going to LA. What will I do there? It's supposed to be violent and expensive. I don't have any money. And what if I fail? How could I come back then? And what if I become a huge success? I'd end up becoming rich and famous for being in films I hate! I'd be a sell-out! Nicholas Hope and Steve Martin in *Father of the Bride III*. Nicholas Hope and Eddie Murphy in *Beverly Hills Cop XIV*. Nicholas Hope with Academy Award winner Mel Gibson in *Terrorist Airforce Patriot*. Isn't that what people go to LA for, to be in those films? Is that what I want? How would I live with myself?

Well, pretty easily. Compromise isn't so hard when you're rich, and it is a real possibility. I have an LA agent now: the door is open. I decide I need advice.

I ask Rolf what he thinks. As usual he gives a noncommittal guru reply. 'Well,' he explains, 'Marty knows what he's doing; he's trying to hit while the iron's hot. There's a lot of talk about you and your performance in *Bubby*. But on the other hand Hollywood will be waiting to see how the film performs, so it's likely you'll have a lot of meetings but no jobs until they know whether you rate as a crowd pleaser or not. So it's up to you.'

That doesn't help. It's not what I want. I want a Go or Stay answer, a solution. The fact is, if I don't go to LA, I have to go somewhere else, do something active about my career. The fading promise of Venice is too depressing to contemplate alone in the flat, dry, pedestrianless streets of Adelaide. It's dismal going every Friday night to one of the two main grungy pubs that my friends frequent. They're within a short walk of each other, on the stretch of Rundle Street that is currently popular. Every Friday, when the first one closes at midnight, the same crowd trudges down to the second, which is licensed until two. What used to be routine fun starts to feel desperate. I have to leave.

I decide on Sydney. That's where most of Australia's Serious Actors live. It's the film capital of Australia, and I'm a film actor now. It makes sense. I mention it to Rolf, just to check his reaction. He's noncommittal. After all, he points out, he moved away from Sydney – Adelaide works well for him – but it's true that most film casting in Australia is done from Sydney. So it's my choice.

Yeah, right.

The bus arrives in Sydney at three in the afternoon. The city is in drought, the air is dry and hot, and the sun is heavy in the sky. Drunks and tramps sit despairingly on the dusty streets around Central Station while I stand amid my luggage, unsure why I'm here.

I've come from the Canberra Arts Festival. Two weeks in a low-ceilinged, fluorescent-lit motel room. Watching plays that left me wondering why I liked theatre. A monologue from a homosexual Australian photographer of Chinese origin who wanted to explain how difficult it was to be all those things, to the accompaniment of slides. The monologue given in a halting, stuttered delivery that was either ill-prepared or stiff with stage fright. I was embarrassed for him, but he got a standing ovation.

The play I was in tackled the subject of racism in small country towns, and had Bad White People versus Good Black People. The Canberra audience gave that a standing ovation as well. The director of the play had cast his wife as one of the leads, but they were in the middle of breaking up with each other so there were backstage fights every night before we went on. It was tiring. And every morning the motel cleaner banged on the door at nine a.m. It just wasn't Venice.

But Sydney might be. I spend the first two weeks at *Confessor Caressor* director Tim Nicholls' place in Paddington. The shops are cosy and fashionable. The people dress well, they drive Mercedes-Benzes and BMWs, they look fit and healthy and well off, and they talk of left-wing politics like it's a close friend. There's a market every Saturday with homemade organic jams and pickles and furniture and jewellery and clothes, with well-dressed buskers, and cafés with coffee and wine and focaccias, and people laughing and smiling and singing. It's comfortable, cosmopolitan. It's as much as I want. I may not have it right yet, but surely I'm tailoring towards it. Just another film or two and I could be here, getting friendly smiles and buying organic produce and discussing left-wing reforms.

But so far, it's way out of my reach.

I move instead into a share house in Glebe, in Sydney's inner west. My room costs as much in rent as a whole house in Adelaide, and it shakes to the volume of traffic on the road outside. Phone messages get lost in the general pile of accumulated papers. One of my housemates has his wardrobe in the living room because it can't fit through the narrow hallway door. I'm having trouble finding an agent.

The house is infested with cockroaches. They are in the toaster, the kettle, the oven, under the fridge. They inhabit the TV set and the rubbish bin and the telephone handset. They fly in through the windows. I can hear them scurrying about at night, their bony, horned legs scratching on the wooden floor.

But I *am* the lead role in a film that won awards in Venice. I *have* to be here if I want to be a Successful Actor in Australia. I have no choice. LA is too scary. LA is too tempting. LA won't work yet because the film hasn't proved itself in the box office. It would be silly to go. Isn't that what Rolf said? And Sydney is the engine room for Australian film. I must be doing the right thing.

And I am, I can tell. I'm starting to get invitations. There's one for the 'Movie Show' Christmas party, SBS Television's end of year bash for its film review program. I don't even know how they found me.

True, I stuff it up. I don't realise it is a catered affair and I bring a bottle of wine with me. Margaret Pomeranz, the host, laughs when she sees it. I think maybe it's the brand, even though I've tried hard. Shit, I've had to budget for it. When the waiters come around I just can't help myself. I don't know anybody so I drink the free wine – free! – and then suddenly realise I've started speaking to people. I end up being sent home in a taxi with a massive cut to the forehead after falling drunkenly into the plate-glass windows of Margaret's house.

But at least I get to meet people. Directors, producers, other actors. Al Clark, who produced some film called *Priscilla*, is there, and Jan Chapman, who produced *The Piano*. And a whole load of others whose names I can't remember. But I can remember talking all night and laughing a lot and waving my arms. I'm sure I've made an impression. I even get an audition from it – a producer phones me up a few days later to ask how my head is and mentions a film he is casting, there is a part for a schizo-phrenic depressive that I might be good for.

And although I may really want to live in Paddington, where the rich, trendy people live and where the dress code is something to aspire to, where surely the cockroaches themselves are cleaner, politer, less obvious, that'll come. It may even be bypassed. If I'm lucky, LA will call me rather than me it, and I'll choose my films. Robert Altman, the Coen brothers, Martin Scorsese, Milos Forman, Steven Soderbergh, Roman Polanski, Peter Weir for local colour.

I just have to be patient and survive the wait. Because *Bubby* is *travelling*. Rolf has just rung and given me another two festivals in tandem. One in some place called Tromsø in Norway, the other in Rotterdam. He tells me I may as well go if I've got the time, it could be interesting, and they've asked for me.

Hell, I've got the time. This is it. How you get seen, right? The only thing I'm going to lose is the dole, but the festivals are feeding me, so if I can cover the rent I'm okay. Maybe I won't even need to come back. Maybe Glebe and the cockroaches and Sydney are just an interim on the way to, well, I'm not sure. Somewhere good.

CHAPTER 3

on top of
the world

Westlands, Whyalla, 1971

Friday night was fish fingers night. No meat on Fridays, we were Catholic. I never liked fish fingers, but they marked the new, exciting boundary between the school week and the weekend. I was 12 and I was becoming an adult. Fish fingers. Friday night. You had to do something or Monday would be hell. I'd finish my homework, eat, change out of uniform, and go.

Forty-five minutes long, dry walk down Nicholson Avenue, away from the scrub lands, past the new housing estate on one side, then Our Lady Help of Christians primary school and church on the other, I'd come to the huge roundabout where Nicholson Avenue divided pie-like into four. Grass had been planted on the roundabout but had never taken. It was still a plate-like desert of red dust in the middle of roasting bitumen. Teenagers with and without driver's licences would race here in their fathers' borrowed cars, using the roundabout as the border from which to speed back to Spencer Street in town again, or else avoiding it and ducking into the car park that took up one whole quadrant of the divided pie. In the centre of the car park, already showing signs of deterioration, was the enclosed shopping mall that had been promised to the migrant population of the western suburbs. Woolworths at one end, Colmarts at the other, a host of 'variety shops' in between, all linked by a single muzak tape. That's where I was headed. Westlands.

On Friday nights, Westlands was open late. Families would do their weekly shopping there, stopping for fish and chips and a cup of tea in the new styrofoam cups at the Colmarts café. By eight o'clock most had finished and gone home to watch 'Play of the Week' or 'The Six Wives of Henry VIII' on the ABC, and the teenagers would be left. It was the only place in the west with a suggestion of city life. You could slouch around looking at everyone else. If you were in a pack, you could wander up and down the mall, laughing at the security staff in their shirts and ties as they tried to follow inconspicuously. If you were on your own, you could try to look cool and unimpressed, browsing through the magazines in the newsagency. But you had to leave just before nine, because once the mall closed and the despised security staff left, the gangs would be milling in the car park looking for entertainment, and if you were still around, you were it. It wasn't really much fun, but it felt right. When people at school asked: 'What'd ya do Fridee night?', you could answer: 'Hung out at Westlands.'

Twelve was the age my parents decided I was safe to walk home alone at night. They were wrong, but I wasn't about to tell them. Dodging the gangs and the dogs that roamed the streets in packs was a dangerous business. They were out there looking for you, and if you were stupid enough to be out on your own, you were fair game. I could usually out-run the gangs, I was fast. The dogs were a different matter. But it was worth it. I'd been waiting to be allowed out on my own for ages. I needed to join in the life of my peers. I needed to give myself some social kudos. My fascination with books and the bush didn't carry much weight at school, they were a negative. And I wasn't old enough yet to think of abnormality as a desired state. I needed something perceived as normal. And on Friday nights, Westlands was a cauldron of displaced puberty. At 12, that was normal.

There was an intense, unsupervised, illicit thrill that came from flicking through the pages of *Men Only* in the Westlands newsagency. An adult thrill. These were pictures of adult desire, and I shared it. I was becoming mature. The excitement of working along the rack of magazines from *Time* to *Newsweek* to *Pix* to *Men Only* was ecstasy in itself. I would become clammy yet confident. I would slouch with studied nonchalance up and down the mall. I began to copy other, popular kids, practise their walks, dress like them. It was a plan of acceptance, a preparation for gang member-ship. My own, private, ongoing initiation ceremony into adulthood.

It was shattered early. On Friday night number six, Westlands was closing and I was about to leave. There was a posse of girls at the exit, all ponchos and slacks and curly hair and ice-creams, and they were watching me approach. It was my new-found confidence, my air of sexual maturity, my practised loucheness. I blushed. Pleasure and embarrassment all at once as I passed them. Then one shouted, 'Hey! Look at the skeleton! Look at him walk!' and the others cackled. It couldn't be me they were talking about. I didn't even turn round, I couldn't. I couldn't let them suspect I thought it *might* be me.

Something hit me in the shoulder. An ice-cream. It stuck, then slid down my arm. The girls were braying with laughter. It cut through the whole of Westlands. People were looking, I couldn't ignore it. I *had* to turn around. They were there right behind me, mimicking my walk, sticking their bums way out behind in a ridiculous swayback position. Oh God is that how I looked?

'What the fuck are you looking at, bitch?' I snarled, trying to be aggressive – they were only girls – but the leader smacked me, closed-fist, in the face.

'Go on,' she taunted, 'I dare you.' And she punched me again. I didn't even see it coming.

'Fuck off,' I began to snarl, 'I'm not going to hit a fucking girl.' But I couldn't get it out, she wouldn't stop pushing. 'Go on,' she said, 'go on, touch me if you dare, you nothing, you skeleton. You walk funny.' And she did the bum walk again and they all laughed and I just ran.

They chased me as far as they could, but they were giggling and laughing so much they ran out of breath and had to stop, which was lucky, I was crying by then.

Humiliation and disappointment and just pure shame. If I couldn't manage the transition to Westlands, how would I ever be accepted in Spencer Street?

'The Six Wives of Henry VIII' was followed by 'Callan', which the whole family would watch. Friday night number seven, and most other Fridays after that, I stayed home to watch with them.

Tromsø, winter 1994

There is a heatwave in Sydney the day I leave. It is over 40 degrees Celsius. I wear sandshoes, a T-shirt and tracksuit pants for the journey, and carry a thin duffle coat. I pack jeans, shirts and R.M. Williams boots for style, pullovers for warmth, and add a jaunty beret to cover my balding, temperature-sensitive head. I try everything on in front of the mirror, and swap some of the shirts. It's casual, but I'm trying for elegant as well. I'm a Sydneysider now.

I've been sunbathing in the cement back garden, doing push-ups and sit-ups. I look browner and fitter than before. I'm ready to make an impression. This time I'm going prepared. Confident, informed, looking as good as possible. I've been to Venice. I know what film festivals are. I know my film is a festival hit. And it's going to be my film, because Rolf won't be there. They've asked for *me*. They've organised my airline ticket and even phoned me at home to check that the arrangements are going to fit my schedule. I'm going to make the most of it, in every way I can. Every way.

This, I've decided, is it. No more hanging back. Time to be a star.

The combined flights to Tromsø take 32 hours, including a three-hour delay in Bangkok. By the time I'm boarding in Oslo, I'm in a daze; the biting cold doesn't quite register. I have to wait in the plane while the wings are de-iced. Great elephantine machines spray toxic-looking foam on to the outside of the aircraft. I'm the only passenger who bothers to watch.

The people around me are very Aryan, yet slightly Asiatic. They have heavy-set faces, slightly narrowed eyes, high cheekbones. They bundle dense, black overcoats and scarves into the luggage racks, read newspapers I can't understand. The language is harsh and unpleasantly seesaw. I am cocooned in solitude.

It is early morning and very dark. When we take off, the city below shines like a small, dainty Christmas card, fairy lights glistening against a backdrop of snow. I float above it, a foreigner in a capsule. The further north we fly, the more severe the landscape becomes. Snow turns to ice, tall mountains rear up one after the other in pristine whiteness, all signs of human habitation disappear. I have no idea what I'm flying into. It's delicious.

The city of Tromsø appears out of nowhere, all the buildings covered in snow. The first visible evidence that it exists are the roads, which have been cleared so that grey bitumen snakes through the snowman-like structures. A massive mountain on one side looms over the city, half of which seems to be built on a peninsula that juts out into the sea and loops round in a semicircle. A bridge connects this part of the town to the other half, on the mainland. There is a 1970s building clearly visible, an A-frame structure made of steel and glass. It glitters. The mountain is icy white, the streets likewise. I'm looking down on something that could be the set of a sci-fi movie.

It is minus 20 degrees Celsius. My baggage has been lost. On the walk to the car my sandshoes freeze. My ears feel like they are burning. Even if my baggage arrives, the R.M. Williams are going to be useless. The pullovers won't do much, either. The beret is woefully inadequate. The man who drives kindly offers to lend me some clothing. He speaks in a sing-song voice, refers to me as Mr Hope, and turns the heater on full blast so it becomes uncomfortably hot. It is still dark and the car slides a little on the ice. The shops we pass have little candles outside the doors.

My hotel room looks out on to the mountain. The sun is just rising and I am so hyperactive from the journey I decide to have a quick shower, then walk around the nearby streets to see what it's like before the jet lag hits or hypothermia sets in. I shower for ten minutes. When I finish it's dark outside. The sun has disappeared. I can't believe it.

The room is so overheated I open the window. The blast of sub-zero air makes me feel intensely awake. Streetlights glow yellow off the snow, and there is a residue of oblique light leaking up from where the sun hides beneath the earth, which gives the air a blue tinge. My body is exhausted but my mind is racing, and all this is so different to the geography of the world I know, there is no way I can sleep. I go to look for Tor, the festival director.

There are things on the way downstairs that I don't recognise. A machine with two roller brushes just near the elevators, another with a dispenser section and plastic cups. I don't know what they are for. People have left their shoes outside the doors of their rooms. I wonder if this is to have them cleaned, and if it costs. The fact that I don't know, that it doesn't matter that I don't know, adds to the exoticism of the snow and the ice and the language.

Tor is sitting in the bar with a couple of other festival staff, and calls me over. I've worked out a plan in advance. I have $100 to share between the two festivals. I have already changed this festival's $50, and received 250 Norwegian kroner in return. I know it won't go far, but I don't want to be seen as stingy. Nobody likes stingy people. And I don't want to appear poor, because that would suggest lack of success. So I offer to buy a round of beers straight away. Beer is cheap, I get to make a good impression, and if I do this now it'll probably be remembered even if I can't do it again. It's a well-known ploy, but I think it can still work.

They refuse, but I insist with great, generous good nature, and they accept. So far so good. 'Four beers,' I say to the barman, holding up four fingers in case he doesn't understand English. He pours, then asks for 180 kroner, in English. That's $36. 'I beg your pardon?' I say. Perhaps I misheard. 'One – hundred – and – eighty – kroner,' says the man, slowly and carefully, so I understand. He's not smiling. It's not a joke.

That leaves 70 kroner for the rest of my stay here. Less than two beers. Fuck knows what everything else costs. I break out in a sweat, standing at the bar wondering if I should give the drinks back, but aware of what that might do to my reputation. What would Rolf do?

He'd be unfazed. If he didn't have the money he'd laugh and explain, and if he did he'd pay up and not mention anything. He's very relaxed about these things, and it works for him. I breathe deeply, take the beers back. They are smiling. I have passed a test. They understand. Tor leans forward, he has something to tell me.

They're giving me per diems! 2500 kroner. 'Beer money,' says Tor. I try not to be too effusive. It'd spoil the image. It's more than three weeks dole in Australia, and makes up for what I'm losing by being away. I suddenly feel relaxed, expansive.

I sit down. I want to know as much as possible about the festival. Who is here, when *Bubby* will show, how many times, what the publicity is, what kinds of activities are arranged. I want to milk this opportunity for all it's worth.

Tor fills me in. It's a small festival. There are three cinemas showing films that are considered unlikely to get a release in Norway. There are various events that centre around eating and drinking. I will meet a few directors from various European countries. And it's a university town so lots of students attend the films.

It sounds good. Not that good, but good. A shame it's small, since I've read in my guidebook that the locals regard Tromsø as the Paris of the north – even though it continues by suggesting that, given the temperatures, the locals may well suffer from cranial frostbite. But who knows, maybe it *is* the Paris of Scandinavia! Maybe there will be parties and groupies and odd Arctic couplings along with adoring European directors. Cranial frostbite could be a plus for a shy Australian actor.

That night there are drinks in Tor's room, a welcome party for today's guests. Meaning me. Tor explains it's the affordable way to drink together, the bar is just for show. There are festival staff, a couple of guests, one or two truculent-looking locals who Tor has taken a fancy to. I end up with the guests and locals, helping ourselves to the free alcohol while Tor sits with his staff on the bed. They discuss the day and other guests who haven't been invited. I listen in, deciding it must be okay to since they're speaking in English and must want to share the information.

They complain about a girl who is trying to sleep with all the foreign directors. They don't approve. And there is a loud, obnoxious American man nobody can place. The makers of the film he is representing deny any knowledge of who he is, and Tor is unsure what to do about him. He can't work out how the man got invited or how to send him back early. He feels foolish about asking him to prove his link with the film. After all, the festival somehow invited him — his name's on the list. It seems he got into the promiscuous girl's bed on his first night. Everyone's very peeved. It's sex on false pretences, they explain. I make a mental note to try to meet her.

After a few drinks, we go out. The buildings are low-level, widely spaced, and vary from ugly 1970s-style utilitarian structures to wooden fairytale houses. It's a cross between a Wim Wenders trailer-trash version of Americana and illustrations from Hans Christian Andersen, with a hint of Kafka thrown in. All this covered by snow and populated by people in furs, gloves, scarves and woolly hats, who strip down to T-shirts and jeans the minute they step inside. Tonight, though, there are groups of teenagers roaming the icy streets, drinking from paper bags, and dressed in T-shirts and jeans. Some of the girls have bare midriffs and wear short skirts. Tromsø, Tor explains, has a huge collection of nightclubs per capita of population. If the teens go early to the nightclub it is free. So they leave their coats in the cloakroom, keeping the tab as proof of entry. And since no one else is there, they wander the frozen streets drinking home-burnt alcohol from bottles in brown paper bags until later, when the nightclub fills up.

It's very familiar, but the cold makes it so extreme – a kind of frost-bitten, frozen-nipple erotica. I'm disappointed when we end up at the festival club with a more adult crowd. I want to see what happens once the frozen teenagers hit the nightclubs and the illegal alcohol hits their thawing bloodstreams. At least there'd be something to look at. Everybody in the festival club is sitting down, drinking beers, smoking, talking Norwegian. Tor has disappeared. I'm on my own. No one has seen the film, no one is talking to me. The smoke is hurting my eyes and lungs. People keep elbowing past me as if they're picking fights. I can feel a slight panic building up and decide maybe I should just go back to the hotel. Once the film is shown things'll surely change.

I wander through the town simply observing, the frozen air hurting my lungs. Chemists here have everything hidden behind the counter. Bottle shops exist as a government-run monopoly with office hours and over-priced booze. People are employed to shovel salt on to the iced-over roads. Hot dogs are the main popular feature sold in American-style

7-Elevens, which are dotted on every corner. Television looks as bad as in Australia but with less adverts. Every second house has a Norwegian flag hanging outside it. There are round, spiral cakes in the bakeries decorated with miniature flags. Bread is cheap but everything else is really, really expensive. There are very few foreigners, and I am one of them. Elbowing people in public places seems to be an acceptable way of negotiating crowds. People become uncontrollably drunk despite the expense. Permanent darkness is depressing.

The festival is popular. Most of the dinners and parties are sold out, and Tor's coterie of truculent locals grows each day. He shepherds them along to functions with paternal charm and leaves them to stand shyly and petulantly in corners, waiting for him to gather them up again. I, too, am becoming impatient and truculent. Two days of solitude in a foreign, non-English-speaking country with no sunlight saps confidence. I want the instant fame that *Bubby* will bring. I'm looking forward to introducing it. I'm depending on it.

When I do finally stand in front of the cinema screen to begin my speech, I see an old acquaintance in the middle of the audience. I can't believe it. It's Natalia! She left Adelaide years ago to join the French circus troupe Arkaos. Maybe Arkaos is in town because of the festival. Of course she'd come to see a film from her home town. I look again. I haven't got my glasses on, but I'm sure it's her, and she is looking at me. This is enticing. Natalia used to be part of a group I always found attractive and elusive. Now she's here, and I'm the star of the film she's come to watch. Our positions are reversed.

Of course all I want to do really is catch up. But then how silly not to go that extra step.

I wave. She doesn't.

It's not her. Of course it's not her. What kind of wish-fulfilment displacement was that? How embarrassing. Waving at the pretty girl in the audience. Of course she was looking at me. I'm about to introduce the film, all the audience is looking at me. How dumb can I get? Tor may think I'm trying to emulate the bed-all-directors girl. He'd be more or less right. I wouldn't mind emulating her. It's part of what I'm hoping the *Bubby* pay-off will be, but I don't want anyone to know. '*Håper dere liken filmer,*' I say, making a jumble of the Norwegian sentence I've been practising so long, but at least they laugh. I continue but forget bits of my speech. It's disastrous. I'm ruining my chances of being seen as the erudite individual I'm working so hard to portray. I need to pull myself together. I round off the introduction as best I can and leave the cinema.

I have nearly two hours before the film finishes, then there will be a small press conference. I decide to brave the ice, go for a walk, settle my thoughts. I head up the hill to see the view.

I do my best to walk carefully. To date I have been so incapable of walking on ice that two people have been assigned to keep me upright whenever I leave the hotel. They operate like guards, taking hold of me under the elbows and sliding me across to the car. I've been grinning forcedly at the indignity of it, slipping like a wounded deer every time they let me go. Whenever that happens they've laughed, amused. I've been trying to ignore it. I don't want to be laughed at. I want to be mobbed. So I'm treading up the hill very slowly and gently, feeling my way forward. I'm determined not to fall.

There are cars totally covered in snow, and the rooftops look like they have frozen waterfalls hanging from them. Snow crackles underfoot. Most other sounds are muffled. There are very few birds or other animals except for the odd dog or cat trying to get inside. People slide down the hill on funny toboggan-like contraptions called sparks, with skis for runners in place of wheels, their shopping dangling in front. One passes by me, a baby in a pouch hanging from its handlebars. The child's arms stick out at right angles from the bulkiness of its clothing, and its bright red cheeks poke out from the hood of its anorak. As the baby passes, arms akimbo, it appears to glide through the air like an ethereal vision. I can sense my equanimity returning.

Everything is peaceful as I cross the road. Then I'm abruptly looking at the sky and smashing down on to solid ice. Winded. In pain. At that instant a bus comes around the corner. The driver sees me and starts trying to stop, but he's having trouble. He's on a downhill, fully frozen slope. I'm trying to get up, but I'm having trouble. I'm on a downhill, fully frozen slope. The bus manages to begin to slow down just inches away, as I use my hands to push my body across the ice towards the footpath. I sit there, trembling, as the driver waves casually and continues on his journey, driving over the beret that marks the spot where my head was. An old woman comes up and says something. I explain I only speak English. 'You should get some spikes for your shoes,' she scolds. 'Stops you breaking bones.' She shows me hers. They look lethal.

I limp carefully back to the cinema, where a room has been prepared in a quite informal way for the press conference. I decide to take control and greet the journalists as they enter, get them onside. I need to do something to help me re-establish the new, sexy, confident image I'm trying to create, that seems to have been so shaken. They look a little surprised by my enthusiasm, and wander off to get tea and coffee before starting any questions. I begin to think that I'm being over-friendly, that I'm anticipating a favourable response, that maybe it's not going to come. Just calm down, I think to myself. Then the fake Natalia walks in.

Close up, she looks nothing like Natalia, and I feel the need to tell her so, to clear this up. I approach her. She stands about an inch taller than me, and she looks a little startled. 'Great film,' she says in a vaguely northern English accent.

I look up at her. 'I'm sorry I waved, I thought you were a friend of mine called Natalia, from Adelaide.' I can feel myself going bright red with the realisation of how gauche this sounds, and redder still with the knowledge of redness. Her eyes go steely grey.

'My name's not Natalia,' she states, 'I'm not from Adelaide.' She moves away and sits down. I nod and look around nonchalantly.

The journalists have taken all the available seats. I am stuck in the middle of a circle of waiting people. It's hard to look nonchalant with everyone staring at me. I blush more. 'Any questions?' I ask brightly, but there is no response. I'm not sure what to do and I'm not confident enough just to wait. I launch into a speech about how I see the film, about some of the specific technical things involved. It works. They start taking notes. One of them interrupts to ask a question. I'm quite proud of myself. I start on a long, technical answer. Halfway through, the girl who is not Natalia leaves.

What have I done wrong? Is she insulted, bored, late for something more important? I want to follow her.

This isn't how it's supposed to be. It should be the other way round.

That night I go to the festival bar again. This time, people are buying me drinks and wanting to talk to me. The *Bubby* effect is in motion. I can hardly move. I'm surrounded by tall men in suits asking me all about the financing and writing of the film. I try to explain I'm just the actor. It is what I wanted, but I'm getting stuck. I want to move around the bar, meet other people. It's not that the men are uninteresting, but really I should mix a bit more, meet a few locals. There's all these women here as well – I'm a star not a producer. I'm backing away from a particularly insistent writer when I bump heavily into someone. It's the non-Natalia. It's my chance. I have to explain.

'I didn't have my glasses on,' I say, 'and you looked like this girl I knew who became a trapeze artist and moved to France, and the guidebook called this the Paris of the north, and my brain just made the link and I waved . . . I'm sorry, but it was exciting to think there was someone I knew out there in an Arctic audience, and then it was mortifying to realise I'd made a mistake, and now it feels like we've already been introduced.'

She laughs.

Bianca. Six feet tall, blue eyes, long hair, slightly tipsy, young, witty, studying in Scotland, willing to talk. This is what I wanted. I have no desire to wander the bar now. She's trying to escape the people she was sitting with, she tells me, one of them's some loud obnoxious American who won't shut up. I ask her what part of England she comes from, and she replies in her distinctly northern English accent, 'Oh no, I'm not English, I'm Norwegian!' I am smitten.

We spend the night talking. When the bar closes we go to my room and drink the bar fridge dry before starting on the one in her room. Thank God for per diems. I want to seduce her or imply that I wouldn't mind being seduced, but it seems the wrong thing to do, we're having such a good time. We've seen the same films, read the same books, had totally divergent backgrounds. What if she's not interested? I don't know how to make that leap and I don't want to stop the talk. It's all gone pear-shaped. I'm supposed to be Star on the Rampage. Instead I'm Infatuated Boy from Australia, sitting on the bed with Girl from Farmland Norway. How did this happen? I'd been envisaging more of a groupie-style sexual smorgasbord in between offers of European work. Isn't that what's supposed to happen to stars?

I invite her into the bathroom to inspect the heated towel rails, they're a novelty to me. There's something about the pristine white tiles and fluffy warm towels that is inspiring. I mention I'd like to kiss her. How idiotic. She looks at me quizzically, pecks me on the cheek, moves on out. I know I've blown it. Then she says, 'My God! It's 8.30!' I don't believe her: it's an excuse, she's lying, it's still dark. Of course it's dark, it's winter: the sun rises about ten and goes down ten minutes later. I have interviews starting at nine. I have to go.

The interviews go really well. I am buzzing. I've got two mini-bars inside me and there's a six-foot Viking still in the building. I can't stop talking. 'You've had too much coffee,' one journalist tells me, 'you should get something to eat.'

There is a function that afternoon hosted by the City of Tromsø for guests of the festival, a feast where everything is made of cod. Cod flesh, cod intestines, cod eggs, cod brain. Even the pavlova-tasting dessert is made of cod. I'm not sure my stomach will manage, but I have to go. Bianca might be there.

The cod is arranged decoratively on a table at the centre of a large room. Guests are seated at smaller tables around it and have to queue up to serve themselves. I walk in and am grabbed by the writer I managed to escape last night. He takes me to sit with his group and they pile my plate with cod delicacies. This is going to be hard. Then I see her. She's at a different table and I'm nervous because she's not looking at me. I try to walk over, but I'm stopped by people who want to talk about the film. I get flustered but attempt not to show it. They have paid to have me here, I have to be courteous. I speak politely about the film, eat slowly, keep glancing at the other table. She's speaking to the man next to her. Who the fuck is he? The woman next to me asks how I am enjoying the meal, and I answer that I'm not used to so many different ways of preparing fish, that I don't think I have had cod before. 'It is not all cod,' she replies and points. 'That is whale.'

I finally manage to get over to Bianca. 'Hello,' I say. She grins. 'How do you feel?' I ask. 'I mean, it was late, I didn't realise –'

'I feel great,' she says.

'Oh,' I say, 'me too, I feel great too, maybe, er . . .' The man next to her interrupts, he's the attaché to the Minister for the Arts and he loved the film. He has a few questions. She stands, she is leaving.

'Tonight?' I say.

'Sure,' she replies.

The attaché wants to know the budget of the film, was it well received, is it a typical Australian film, how well has it sold?

'The hotel bar?' I say.

'Seven,' she replies.

It takes forever to get to seven. It takes forever to get past the drinking and subterfuge to the main question: DidI-blowitlastnightinthebathroomoraretheremorekissestocome?

She looks surprised. I change tack. 'I know there's only

a limited time,' I say. I sound like a self-help book. 'But if we're agreed, it could be such a *special* limited time.'

I blush. I'm not comfortable with sentiment. I'm not comfortable with bluntness. I'm not comfortable.

'Of course,' she says, matter-of-factly. 'I thought that's what we were doing.'

We spend the next two days together. It is fabulous. *Everything* is fabulous. *I* am fabulous, *she* is fabulous, *we* are fabulous together. The frozen mountain outside my window positively glows, the heated towel rails stay full of allure, the bar fridge keeps being filled, we never make it down to breakfast. I float on teenage air. It's exactly where I wanted to be. It is the only place I wanted to be. How did I not know?

On the morning we have to leave, she goes three hours before me. The air is blue with cold.

It's not, of course. It's blue with refracted light. But I'm shell-shocked, I want to think like that. And I'm on my way to Rotterdam. Another festival, another party, another *Bubby* success. It's hard, I think to myself, but I may have to get used to these kinds of bittersweet partings.

Rotterdam, winter 1994

Ugly. That's how it looks. Empty, concrete squares surrounded by utilitarian, tower-block offices. But I don't
know, maybe they're flats, maybe people live in them. And
it's cold in a different way, all damp and not so much biting
as seeping. It gets into your bones, makes you aware of how
lonely you are. How could anyone want to be here? There's
no snow to make it look beautiful or to soften the structures, just drizzle and sludge. I don't want to be here. I want
to be back there. When I'm picked up at the airport the
driver doesn't talk, just takes me to the hotel reception and
points to the desk that is surrounded by people. I join the
queue. No one there talks to me, either.

There are hundreds of films showing and hundreds of
guests. It's going to be hard to make an impression. I book
in, go to my room. It's big. It looks out on to an empty
square with a fountain in the middle that isn't working. It
doesn't have the pizazz of the frozen mountain view I've
come from. My desire lingers back there.

Stop it! I think. Keep active, make the most of *this*
festival. Overcome this lovelorn somnambulation, it's
threatening to blanket your chances of success. It was a
fling. Get a grip on yourself.

I make my way to the publicity desk to see what's
in store. It's in a room crammed full of journalists
and guests. They're all smoking. I can hardly breathe. The
desk has another queue. People are picking up reams of
faxes, making appointments, shouting at the publicity
staff because they can't book an interview or fit in a

screening. It should be exciting, but all I feel is overwhelmed.

The woman who serves me asks for my name, and whether I'm here as a journalist or with a film. I'm taken aback. 'I'm with the film *Bad Boy Bubby*,' I answer. 'From Australia. I've just flown in from Tromsø, I –'

'Yes,' she interrupts, flicking through a folder. 'We have you listed. You can pick up your registration in the office across the hall.'

'Well, yes,' I say, 'but have you got an itinerary for my interviews?'

She looks briefly at her listings. 'No one has asked for an interview,' she says. 'We'll let you know if they do.'

I'm shocked. There must be some mistake. *Bubby* is a festival hit and it's already been screened for the press here – surely someone wants to interview me. 'Are you sure?' I ask. 'I mean, I'm willing to do as much publicity as you want.'

'We'll let you know,' she answers. 'Now please, there's a queue, I am busy.'

I don't know what to do. I'm just in the way. All around me is this picture of vibrant, frantic film activity that doesn't involve me. I have to be seen to be active.

I could go for a walk outside. I could disappear to my room. I could register. The three options seem equally shaky at this point, but the room is winning until I'm grabbed by the elbow and asked if I'm Nicholas Hope. 'Yes!' I shout. The woman introduces herself. I don't catch her name, but she works for the Dutch distributors who are releasing *Bubby*. Can I meet them for breakfast tomorrow? 'Thank God,' I sigh, and go to register.

It's a long day until tomorrow's breakfast. I use my registration card to go and see some films, but there's nothing I like. I go to the main meeting place, an open bar on one of the hotel floors, and stand alone, breathing in cigarette fumes and feeling awkward. There's a lot happening out there other than educated lung cancer, but I'm not part of it. No one even looks at me. I'm worried – I know the film has already screened once, I should be besieged. I can see other people being hounded, fending off admirers or press or whoever it is they're fending off. I can't understand what's gone wrong.

My anonymity is growing, I can see my isolation glancing off the walls. I should force myself to mingle. I can't help thinking how much better it might be if Bianca were here. Tromsø was certainly easier. Maybe I should approach this festival the same way. I look around to see if there are any potential Rotterdam Biancas in the crowd, but no one fits. My responses are locked into a six-foot, blue-eyed, northern-English-accented Norwegian genetic code.

I go to the festival reception area and ask how much it costs to ring Norway. It sounds expensive. I look around, but all the phones are taken, so I sit down on a couch to wait for one to become available. Suddenly the thought of making a phone call to Norway becomes ridiculous. What on earth will I say? I stand abruptly, knocking a table, and leave the room. I'll go for a walk.

One post-modern block away from the hotel and all the signs of the festival disappear. I can't even see any posters. I keep walking in a straight line so as not to get lost, and stop when I reach a highway. I turn around and head back.

Dinnertime. There is a smorgasbord that we help our-selves to, and I do. I toy with the idea of sitting with other people and introducing myself but decide against it. I have no idea what I might follow the introduction with. I find an unoccupied table and sit there instead. Someone walks by and smiles at me, handing me a flyer. Maybe they recog-nise me. It's an advert for a film. They want people to go. What the hell, I think, I've nothing else to do.

There are two other people in the cinema. One of them is the person who gave out the flyer. The film is tedious and I think the flyer person is the lead character, but if so he has a bad wig on. At the end, there's only me and the flyer person left in the cinema, and he doesn't look like he wants to be approached.

Back at the hotel, the meeting room is unbreathable and buzzing. I pass it in the elevator on the way to my room. Other guests get out on that floor, stale-tobacco smoke gusting through the closing doors. I wheeze my way up the next few levels. There's no way I'm going to even try to mingle in such a self-centred morass of other people's stinking nicotine addiction. Who do they think they are? Have they no manners, no class?

I should at least have had a drink in the bar, I think to myself. Something to make me feel like I'm at a festival, like I'm trying. I could have something from the mini-bar. I open it. It's all arranged neatly, in expensive lines. No, I think, that's too sad. It's too sad to drink from the mini-bar on my own.

Morning. The distributors are arranging publicity. I have interviews with newspapers, TV, magazines, a live question-and-answer session. As if I ever doubted it. Why can't I be more confident? And if I'm going to be confident, why not gratify everything? Why not admit I am infatuated, love-sick, teenage? Is that not as much of a fairytale reality as the clichéd rock'n'roll Hollywood one I was dreaming of under the sun in Glebe?

I ring Norway.

A woman answers the phone in Norwegian.

'Is it possible to speak English?' I ask.

'Of course it is,' she replies, in a highly cultivated accent.

'I'm looking for Bianca. Is it possible to talk to Bianca?'

'Who will I say is calling?'

'Nicholas, my name is Nicholas.'

There is a pause. I can hear the telephone money clicking away.

'Hello?'

'Bianca?'

'Yes. Hello?'

'It's me, Nicholas.'

There is a pause. Maybe this was a bad idea.

'We met in Tromsø.'

'Yes, I remember. I wasn't *that* drunk.' She laughs. 'It's good to hear from you.'

'Ha, yes, well I just thought that maybe it's a silly idea but even so we seemed to get on so well and now I'm just in Rotterdam and it's another festival and I thought that maybe you could come here as well.'

She doesn't say anything. It's awful. I rush into the chasm.

'I have some per diems, I could help with the fare, if you got here tomorrow we'd have four days . . . It could be really good. It's really big.'

Another terrible pause. Then she answers.

'I was thinking about university, but that doesn't start for another week or two.'

University? I'd forgotten the youth bit. Ah well . . .

'I'd like to see you again. I think I can come.'

Imagine that. Would I have had the courage to give the same answer?

'I don't know about you paying, it all sounds a bit rushed. We'll talk about that later,' she says.

Well, there you go, she's very *mature* for someone so young . . .

The next day when she arrives I start to bubble again. It's unbelievable that she's here. It's a different *country*, for God's sake, and she just came over. Is it me she's here for or the chance of a free festival? Me, I decide, me. We meet in that foyer section with the smokers and all the people talking to each other, and she just melds in. The first conversation she has is in three languages at once – I haven't even managed to have a conversation in one. We meet the actor Steve Buscemi, attend parties, go to dinner with an Australian director called Clara Law. Bianca does most of the talking. I try to focus on career building, but my hormones get in the way. I keep giggling, drink too much, go moony-eyed. I'm not sure what to say to Steve, how to act at parties, whether or how to impress Clara. I realise it's a form of chemical insanity, but it's too compelling to control. She might be young – shit, I was a *teenager* when she was born – but right now I feel that this time is all that counts. It's glorious.

The interviews I had wanted so much before are now in the way. I'm conducting one with a New York journalist who is giving me his details, offering to do anything he can to get *Bubby* released in the States or to help me if I come over. When he asks, 'So, who's the girl?', it surprises me. It's a personal question. I don't like to think of her as a girl. I hesitate. 'Oh come on,' he says, 'I just want to know. You're with her all the time.'

'We met in Tromsø,' I explain. 'She's come here to join me.'

'Oh,' he laughs dismissively, 'a festival romance. You'll get used to it.'

I know I won't. I know I won't because I don't want to leave. I've no interest in chasing a US release. I can't be bothered with any help this journalist says he can offer me. In fact, I'm insulted that he questions my emotional state. How dare he? Doesn't he understand I'm just interested in being in the hotel room with the non-functioning fountain out the window? Doesn't he realise I got invited to a major party by the distributors who wanted to introduce me to a producer *and I forgot to go* because this feeling is more real than any *film* release? Yes, I've succumbed to my hormones and emotions and I know they're linked – but this is such a short-lived thing, we both go back to opposite ends of the earth in a few days, we have to make the most of it. Can't he see that? How can he be so smug? Surely Rolf can chase the States. I'll hand the details on, I'm busy. Maybe I shouldn't even go back. Sydney's just Sydney, all sun, open spaces, brashness and cockroaches. I don't fit in, I should go somewhere else, somewhere like . . . Norway, for instance. It's bound to have a film industry, wasn't Ingmar Bergman from there? No, says Bianca, that's Sweden.

We have four days.

As I come through passport control in Sydney, a young official with a Tin Tin haircut smiles and says, 'G'day, welcome back.' It's a grating, hard-to-understand accent. The sun is harsh and unfriendly on my skin. There's no work and no one's even heard of the film. I'm sent on a go-see to the 'C for Casting' casting agency, who tell me I should get a toupee if I want to act in Sydney, there's not much call for bald men. They check my hands in case they can be used for an advert. They have no idea.

I take to sitting in the cement backyard in Glebe, wondering how far Sweden actually is from Norway. If I keep to the backyard I may be able to save enough for a fare.

Rome, summer 1994

It's so much slower than I thought. Rolf had told me as much. He'd said not to expect anything, that the film already had a life bigger than anticipated. But I'm inclined to want to believe other people, the ones who tell me I'm going to be a star, and I'm getting impatient. Yes, yes, I remember Rolf asking me if that was really what I wanted, but how do I know if I don't try?

There'd been a South African producer who was thinking of buying *Bubby* for North American release who had phoned me, and asked me to meet him at the departure lounge in Sydney Airport on his way through. It cost me $30 in taxi fares but Rolf said it was probably worthwhile, you've got to spend money to make money.

'You,' said the South African producer, looking into my eyes, 'are going to be huge.' Six months later he'd decided not to buy the film. Thirty dollars of wasted investment, and I'm still not huge.

Okay, so I have had parts in other films. *The Life of Harry Dare*, directed by Alexis Vellis, and *Exile*, by Paul Cox. Totally different to *Bubby*. I wasn't the lead, and the parts were small. And the filming was more tied to a schedule than to a linear narrative. Now, on the one hand, these roles have allowed me to consider myself a Film Actor, but on the other, I'm unsure what the final product will be like. If I'm not very good in them it might just mean that I'm not very good. But then again, it might just mean I'm not very good at small parts. I can think of lots of actors I like who I haven't seen in small roles. Maybe they're not very good in small parts, either. At any rate, it hasn't helped. I'm still on the dole, I'm still in share-hell cockroach house, I'm still on the other side of the world from my Fantasy Star Affair.

But now, finally, more than half a year after Venice, things are moving. *Bad Boy Bubby* is opening in Italy. That's where I am, sitting exhausted after another 32-hour trip from Sydney to a new resort that is on the south-eastern coast of the country and is either run or owned by Domenico's family. I've been given a suite of rooms and told to help myself to anything, to make whatever phone calls I need, to join the family for dinner at ten but to feel free to come for drinks any time. I might be tired, surrounded by inherited wealth, isolated by language, but I'm totally won over by luxury, free products and free alcohol.

There's a depressed artist who is painting murals on the stuccoed walls surrounding the resort. She's just broken up with her husband. We flirt in broken English. Proof, I tell myself, that I'm getting over my Bianca infatuation, getting ready to continue with career building. I spend the next two days lolling semi-casually in a state of mild inebriation around the half-painted walls, talking about modern relationships, the difficulty of commitment, the nature of love and artistes. I could get used to this.

Then the publicity tour starts. I get packed on to the train to Milan. The flow of alcohol and melodrama stops.

I am looked after by a woman called Carolina. We met before when I was last in Italy, and she says she wants me to have a good time, she remembers the stories of Empty Adelaide that I told her. I'm surprised – I didn't know I had. I follow her around all day. We step on the testicles of a bull drawn on the pavement in the middle of the city for luck. We climb to the top of a spired cathedral. We get an exclusive, free tour of La Scala Opera Theatre.

Over coffee and sandwiches on the balcony of her friend's flat, Carolina asks what my first impressions are.

'Well,' I say, 'it's very lively. But what's hit me the most is how incredible people look. Especially the women. Everyone is dressed fabulously, everyone looks chiselled – the city looks like it's populated by models.'

Silence.

'It is hard to get jobs if you don't look like a model,' says Carolina, tersely. Her friend nods once. I want to say that *they* look like models, but I gather it wouldn't go down well.

'Women in Milan, women in Italy, spend a great deal of their income on clothing and make-up,' she continues. 'They have to, to compete. It is not good. Italy is not a good place for women.'

She turns away. More silence. Rolf should be here.

We sit until it is time for the interviews. Carolina and her friend speak together, quietly, in Italian. I look out on to the street below. Everybody looks fabulous.

When I get to Florence there is a tall, dapper-looking man in a finely tailored linen suit waiting for me. He ignores my extended hand and looks drily at my luggage before gesturing at me to follow. I run struggling behind him with two full cases, trying to keep up with his breakneck pace through the crowd. He drives me to the most elegant hotel I have ever seen, waits at reception while I drag my baggage from the car, then hands me a publicity schedule written in Italian, and leaves. The only thing he has said in all this time is my name: 'Neekolas Ope?' I don't see him again.

I don't much care. The hotel is exquisite. I wish I had more than one night. I wish I lived here. There's a full bookcase across one wall, in wood that I think might be mahogany. There's no TV that I can see. There are rich, maroon, velvet drapes hanging from the bay windows. There is a massive four-poster bed.

I've never slept in a four-poster bed. I've never done anything in a four-poster bed. I wish I had a companion to share it with. What about the journalists I'm supposed to meet? Perhaps one of them will be accommodating. Is that such a wild fantasy? Isn't that what people expect?

I meet the journalists at a late-night garden dinner in the hotel's sylishly landscaped courtyard. They are polite but restrained. They are concerned about the cat. Very concerned. I had forgotten. I try to explain the problem of feral cats in Australia, to justify the film's abuse of the animal by defining it as dangerously foreign. There is an uncomprehending, disapproving silence.

The Florence reviews are scathing about the treatment of animals in the film. The distributors fret. They, too, had been worried about the cat. 'Italians,' they say, 'love their cats. We thought you could talk about how the cat was treated well.'

'But it wasn't,' I explain. 'I'm a bit ashamed.'

'Perhaps,' they advise, 'you could try to hide your shame.'

Bloody Rolf, I think, it's his fault!

Lucia is at the station in Rome. Lucia is the woman Marty wanted me to 'make a move on' in Venice. She's part of Intra Films, the sales agents for *Bubby*, and she's helping with the release. I am unsure what I think of her.

She and a friend were with Domenico when I was picked up at the airport. They came on the four-hour drive to the seaside resort as well. I was tired. The flight had been hell. Twenty-eight hours from Sydney to Rome with two long stopovers on a stuffed economy-class plane with screaming children, screaming parents, frequent terrifying turbulence, and a very surly crew. I hadn't slept. No one told me the drive would be four hours long. My spine was atrophying, my knees just wanted to stretch, my whole body wanted silence and a bed.

Lucia and her friend spoke loudly for the whole trip, in English, so as not to be rude. They compared the features of their different holiday houses in Sardinia: how many bedrooms, size of gardens, number of facilities. Lucia complained about the size of her house in Rome. It was too small, she was going to have to sell and buy another, but that meant she'd have to wait for the property market to somehow favour both the sale and the purchase. Life is so difficult. Her friend agreed. I wanted to tell them about the cockroach-infested house I was renting with two others in Glebe, about the cramped economy seat, about being on the dole, but held back. They might have thought I was jealous. Envious. Ungrateful.

And here Lucia is at the station. It's lucky I said nothing. She waves as I get off the train, then gives me a hug. I hug her back.

She drives me to my next hotel, talking all the while about the upcoming schedule. I don't hear. I'm too scared. She is weaving recklessly in and out of traffic, jumping red lights, mounting the footpath with horn blaring, screaming abuse at other drivers who are in her way. She screeches to a halt in front of the hotel. I ask why she pays no attention to the lights or road markings. 'Oh Neekolas,' she replies in a sexy, husky, rich voice, 'those things, they are just hints for drivers.'

That night there is a reception in the hotel bar for the British contingent of some alternative arts festival being held in Rome. Actor Tilda Swinton and director John Maybury are there. I recognise Tilda Swinton from the film *Orlando*. Oh my. I am introduced to them both. Oh my! I smile but don't say anything. I'm starstruck. They open up their circle of British dignitaries to include me. I'm surrounded by people with mellifluous voices and impossibly relaxed body language. They look at home in their tuxedos and tweeds. They smell of old leather and cigars. They laugh gently at jokes I've probably missed the set-up for, from birth. I'm tongue-tied with the reignition of a class-based inferiority complex.

Class-based? Well, it's easier to think of it like that.

Maybury has a film showing with Swinton as the only character. It's a monologue about a woman who survives the Nazi regime by taking on the uniform and character of her dead husband, a Nazi soldier. I love it. I want to be in it. I want to work with them both, but I can't even make an intelligible comment. My vocabulary has gone, my voice sounds uncouth in my ears. I mumble a clumsy 'Well done!' with overawed embarrassment. They invite me to join them on the roof terrace the next day for drinks. I bubble with gratitude. My sycophancy sickens me, but I just can't thank them *enough*. I'm also worried. They're talking about ordering wine from room service, which is bound to be terribly expensive, and I'm too embarrassed to mention it. They don't sound like the sort of people who talk much about money.

I didn't even know there was a roof terrace. But there it is, overlooking the whole city and drenched in sunlight, with a small pool off to the side. How come nobody told me? Tilda and John, as I now haltingly call them, are sitting with two semi-naked, good-looking men with equally suave British accents. One of them looks familiar. They don't introduce themselves, so Tilda does. Rupert and someone whose name I don't catch. Rupert nods dismissively and continues talking about the benefits of doing poorly paid theatre work for the occupants of Glasgow tenements. They really appreciate it, he comments, that's where it's at. It doesn't sound right to me, I can feel my neck hairs bristling. I wonder to myself how his cultivated voice goes down over in the tenements but don't comment. I can't see Rupert in there. He wouldn't last a second. And the hotel roof terrace is far better.

Tilda mentions that she and her husband may have to move out of London and back up to Scotland because of finances. I start to think maybe I'm judging the accents too harshly. We all sip our wine. John asks what I am here for, so I tell him and invite him to a screening. Rupert wanders off languorously halfway through the telling to put suntan lotion on the other guy. Rupert's in films, says John, you may have seen him in *The Comfort of Strangers*. Oh yes, I say, I thought he looked familiar.

Something about the feel up here keeps the inferiority complex very present. I'm not sure what. Maybe it's just the poise with which they accept all this luxury, the way their bodies flow into it. Maybe it's their unquestioning air of confidence. At any rate, although I'm gushingly excited when they ask me to join them on a visit to the Sistine Chapel tomorrow, and although I desperately want to be their friend and do what they do, I make an excuse not to attend. 'I've got an interview at midday,' I tell them. I want them to realise my film is important, too. 'Besides,' I continue, 'I've been before, when I was backpacking.' There's a slight hiccup of silence after that word, before the conversation continues.

The next morning I go for a walk, still wondering if I should have gone with them. I'm uncomfortable. Alone, stiff in my body, out of place in this world of arty people seemingly born to the job. It's a self-imposed feeling, I tell myself. It doesn't help.

I turn a corner and suddenly see a huge wall of my own image. Posters of my face, larger than life, arching down the street. I am embarrassed. And elated. I think about turning back. Instead, I walk slowly down the street beneath the posters. I lean on the wall. People look at me curiously, unable to marry the image with the diminutive reality beneath it.

I can, I want to tell them. What I am is walking diminutively down the street. What I could be, want to be, should be, is up there, huge and dominating on the wall.

The interview is really good, the journalists laugh at my jokes, and Domenico takes me back to his office to give me a script of a short film he wants to direct, with me in the lead role and Francesca Neri as the lead woman. Francesca Neri, famous Italian star, and me. Acting together. Two other directors are there waiting for meetings with Domenico. Both take me aside and tell me they want to work with me. One has a role for a mute who commits suicide, the other wonders how quickly I could learn Italian. How simply my confidence is restored. The world is opening up to me. I too will soon easily accept the rooftop terraces of free hotels and discuss the merits of theatre for the working classes from the vantage point of a deckchair by the swimming pool. It's all within reach.

Bubby is the winning lottery ticket, I've just got to work out how to cash it in. I agree to the short, I agree to the mute suicide, I profess a love of Italian. It's so easy.

I spend the rest of the day wandering round the city of Rome. There's the Forum, the fashion shops, the Spanish Stairs, the Colosseum, that street with the posters of me, that street again, then a meeting with Domenico and his friends in a small restaurant for dinner. Two of them are organising a riverboat women's film festival along the Danube. They have friends and collaborators visiting from America and Germany. The conversation is engrossing, uplifting. My contribution is witty and entertaining – I can tell, people laugh. I drink red wine with Domenico's friends late into the night. That feeling of inferiority is gone.

The next day is my last in Rome, and I've arranged to meet an old Adelaide acquaintance, Marcello, who lives here. He drives me to the outskirts of the city on a tour of Mussolini's fascist architecture. We stand in the middle of an amphitheatre, surrounded by sculpted representations of Aryan masculinity, and reminisce about our days in Adelaide. Marcello would like to return, if only to visit. 'I need to check,' he explains. 'Rome seems so big, so cosmopolitan when you first visit, so full of life. But it's really just another small city, just another set of provincial attitudes, just another European capital with a seething undertow of right-wing hatred and left-wing hopes.' He smiles.

I'm still exuberant on hazy promises, and about to leave for another festival in Seattle. I don't have to think about

Australia or Europe or provincialism or right and left wings or even cockroaches for another week or so. I can continue in a state of suspended animation. Marcello's dilemma doesn't touch me. I'm in another world. Adelaide, I think to myself, is no comparison.

Seattle, summer 1994

Rolf has unwittingly collected a groupie and is giving her advice. She's one of the production coordinators for the Seattle Film Festival, and she's asking for hints about writing. He is explaining that if her passion is to write films then that is what she should do. She shouldn't help organise film festivals because that is simply a distraction. He speaks with the guru calm that is his trademark, and doesn't notice that she visibly wilts every time he looks at her, which is often. She tells me later that he is a Special Person, that Goodness and Talent radiate from him. I listen politely, wondering if I should tell Rolf later or let it slide. I am unsure if he really doesn't recognise the nature of these attentions or if he simply chooses to be seen not to recognise them. And I'm jealous. I want to be the star.

She interrupts my musings. 'Did I tell you about Rutger?' she asks.

'Rutger? *Blade Runner* Rutger?' I say.

'Yes,' she replies, 'the replicant robot.'

I shake my head.

'I introduced them,' she continues. 'I said, "Rutger Hauer, this is Rolf de Heer. Rolf directed the film *Bad Boy Bubby*, which is showing at the festival." And you know what Rolf said?'

'No,' I answer.

'Well, he looked at Rutger, then at me, then at Rutger, and said, "And what do you do, Rutger?"' She smiles at me. Her eyes are puppy-wet. 'He didn't know who Rutger Hauer was,' she says. 'Isn't that great?'

'I suppose it has its charm,' I respond.

We have a press dinner in something which seems to be called The Needle and which looks like Centrepoint Tower in Sydney. Perhaps, I think, lots of cities decided to build these structures as tourist attractions, more sophisticated versions of the Big Pineapples, Big Lobsters, Big Bananas and Big Everythings that dot Australian country towns. The view is expansive. Seattle kind of oozes out into the distance. The buildings look all low level and, from this vantage point, temporary – a kind of extensive, sprawling trailer park. Lots of people at the dinner introduce themselves and compliment me in an American accent on my performance in *Bad Boy Bobby*, then tell me sincerely that this is the home of grunge, that Nirvana started here, that I will like Seattle. I already don't, but I can see how the relationship between grunge and trailer park could develop. It takes me some time to realise that my interest is assumed because of the grunge band in *Bubby*. I wonder if people here talk to Rutger about robots.

It's a popular festival and there are a lot of unofficial parties attended by the same people. Volunteer workers drive us to houses and flats overflowing with festival guests, the locals trying to work out if anyone famous has turned up in the latest delivery. It's hard to keep track of time and place. We keep being moved. We festival guests are the volunteer workers' party ticket. It reminds me of when I used to be in a punk band in Adelaide, the feel is the same. It's that whole teenage angst but dragged on a few years. There is desperation in the air, a need to be rebellious but popular, to be bigger than your frowned-upon origins. 'Selling out' is the biggest sin, getting out the biggest desire. It feels like home except I have an advantage: I'm a star from outside. I'm not quite Hollywood, but I'm still a hot party entrant. One man, hearing that I'm from Australia, asks me if I know Nicholas Hope, star of *Bad Boy Bobby*. 'It's Bubby,' I tell him, 'and yes, I know him well.' It is enough. He calls his girlfriend over. 'This guy,' he says, 'knows Nicholas Hope!'

Most of the festival guests I meet are young American directors, earnest and intense and unfailingly male, accompanied by their nervous actress girlfriends. There is a rash of contemporary gangster films being shown, and these people have made them. I get attention for being Bubby, I get invited to stay if I'm ever in LA, but it's Rolf as writer/director who is the epicentre – and he's not interested. It's making me grumpy. People at parties keep asking me where he is. I'm beginning to sympathise with all those wives of famous people. 'He doesn't like these kinds of functions,' I reply with spite, 'or the people who go to them. He finds them facile.'

It's the same at the official dinners. I'm all politeness to film directors Whit Stillman and Ang Lee, both promoting their latest films, both potential employers. I get to sit next to Mr Lee. I want him to remember me, and give me a job. I start by saying how exciting it must be for him to follow his films around the world. He tells me no, he misses his wife and family, this is the beginning of what will probably be a year of promotional touring. He hates it, he is lonely.

I don't know how to continue. 'I'll be your friend' doesn't seem appropriate. We sit in silence.

Mr Stillman, meanwhile, is sitting with Rolf. He is laughing. He's telling Rolf that he always attends every festival screening of his films, to judge the response, but then each time someone moves or leaves, he experiences an attack of nerves, accompanied by severe nausea. I'm listening in and I laugh along to show I'm interested and in sympathy, but Whit doesn't notice. He's more interested in Rolf. How did Rolf get jolly Whit and I get depressed Ang? Rolf responds in kind to Whit's story by recounting the time he checked on an Adelaide screening of his film *Dingo*, featuring Miles Davis, and was told that only two people had bought tickets but they'd gone into the wrong cinema. They'd seen *The Commitments* instead. As the audience came out, he overheard two old ladies complaining that they hadn't expected so much swearing, and didn't think the music was at all jazz. Whit laughs. Rolf laughs. They both laugh together.

I laugh, too, just a little too loud. I need to be seen to be relaxed about this story, but I'm not. Self-deprecation is all very well, but there's a time and a place. I want Whit to think of Rolf as a major filmmaker, an arthouse audience pleaser. The kind of filmmaker who uses actors Whit might be interested in looking at. Rolf should be more careful about what, and who, he chooses to tell. It's a question of loyalty. What about me?

And Rolf's adherence to honesty over loyalty doesn't end there. Seattle works on a popular vote, and Rolf's groupie asks if we would like to fill out a box of forms voting our film as the best in all categories. 'We can't do that,' says Rolf. 'Why not?' she says. 'Everyone else does.' She points out one of the other directors sitting in a corner by the ballot box with a pile of forms. 'You should do it,' she says. 'You could win.' Rolf looks at me and raises his eyebrows questioningly.

I hate it when he does that. I don't want the responsibility, I don't want my ethics put to the test. If Rolf weren't here I'd fill them all out and photocopy a load more, but I can't let Rolf down. More to the point, I can't let myself down in his eyes. It's so frustrating, I don't know if the payoff of being good in front of Rolf is worth not winning. I don't even know if Rolf is that concerned. We decline. 'Well,' she says, 'I'm not going to do them *all*.'

I sneak down later that afternoon to get an armful of forms, but the voting has closed. We lose best film and best actor by a couple of votes each. Rolf shrugs. 'Well,' he says, 'she obviously did quite a few. Just not enough.' I nod and laugh. Why do I do that? I would have liked to win best actor. All we had to do was fill out a few measly forms. Everybody does it, why not us? I'm seething inside but I'm too embarrassed to say. I can see him looking at me, and can imagine his response if I raised the issue: You could have filled out the forms, Nicholas, we would always have known how we got the result, if that was okay by you then that was your decision . . . and so on. Damn damn damn damn, the man's turning into my conscience.

The closing party is like a school dance. Everyone is

trying to pick up everyone else. The American accents and sexual desperation that fill the room make me feel like the oddity in the middle of a Hollywood teen flick. Suddenly I want to be back in Tromsø. There is a screening of the volunteer workers' favourite film. It is *Bubby*. The party audience is drunk and screaming, 'Saran Wrap! Saran Wrap!' They are screaming about the gladwrap used in the film, but they've chosen to use the American term for it. I'm fascinated. This is a different cultural experience: everyone here seems to be mentally ten years younger than their bodies. They're falling over, mauling each other, standing up in their seats to copy the actions on screen, spewing in the aisles. It's like their hormones came late. Rolf's groupie finds me and asks if I know where Rolf is. 'Asleep,' I answer. 'He hates these kinds of functions.' She nods, disappointed, takes my arm firmly and leads me away towards the elevator. 'It's a bit ugly,' she says. 'You don't want to see.'

CHAPTER 4

brushing the tip of fame

St Luke's, Whyalla, 1973

Grey shirt, grey shorts or trousers, black shoes, grey socks, green and gold tie, green and gold blazer. The tie was mandatory even in summer when the temperature soared to 110 degrees Fahrenheit. The Brothers were so adamant on this point I'd get nervous if I saw a police car on the way to school, thinking they'd get me for not having my tie on. The classrooms were small, without airconditioning, and after lunchtime they would stink of sweat, soggy sandwiches and hormones. It was a pretty basic school, but it had high academic results for Whyalla.

The building was constructed in the shape of a crucifix. You could just make it out if you stood on top of Baron Hill and looked down at the school laid out before you. Six classrooms made up the foot of the cross – grades 6 and 7, then years 1, 2, 3 and 4. There was an outdoor seating area underneath the classrooms, and a tuck shop where you could buy lunches of meat pies, pasties, sandwiches made with Smith's Crisps, kitchener buns and lollies. The arms of the cross were the offices for the headmaster and the secretary on one side, and the library on the other. Then the head was the chapel, and the living quarters for the Catholic Brothers and the caretaker. It worked as a kind of status ladder, a toes-to-head degree of importance. Below this building, which was placed a little way up the hill, was the just-seeded red oval, and below that Steel Avenue, baking in the sun.

It was an all-boys' school. The girls were catered for by the nuns further up the road, at St Stephen's, where my sister was having a hard time. On her first day she got into trouble for befriending a girl who no one was supposed to be talking to. She'd been raped, and the nuns thought she'd be a bad influence on the others.

The Catholic Brothers at St Luke's weren't nearly as rigid as that. By the time we were 11, we'd been taught all about reproduction. The class had demanded a lesson, sticking questions in the weekly question box designed to embarrass the teacher. Things like 'How does your cock get stiff?' and 'What is a Head Job?'. Brother Dixon drew a diagram on the blackboard of the male and female bodies in cross-section, and explained the mechanics of making babies. We learnt that women gave birth through the anus, even though there were no connecting tubes in the diagram. 'Women's bodies change at these times,' Brother Dixon explained.

When we were 14 we had The Ox, so called because of

his habit of tightening his lips and snorting through his nose when angry, and because of what some of the footballer boys said about the size of his penis. It didn't occur to me to ask how they knew, I assumed they were just making it up, that they said it because The Ox was huge, an ex-body-builder he claimed. But later it came out that they had a more intimate understanding. I'd always wondered why they were called up to the desk when the rest of the class had to write an essay, why they stood so close, how they got the best marks. Why they were allowed to put *Playboy* and *Penthouse* double-page spreads on the class notice board. 'A woman's body is a beautiful thing,' The Ox said when he first saw them, and crossed his legs. I remember that bit, I had to cross my legs too. Half the class had crossed legs and the other half was in rotation up at The Ox's desk. But that was it until Parents' Day, when The Ox made the favourite boys take the naked, sultry women down. 'It'll give the wrong impression,' he explained.

Me and The Ox didn't get on much. We had arguments in class about the Vietnam War and the White Australia Policy. The Ox thought conscientious objectors were just cowards, and that the White Australia Policy had no lasting effect on Australian immigration. I argued differently – not that I knew anything about it, I was just quoting my elder siblings. But The Ox would purse his lips, snort through his nose, and *thwack*! he'd hit the desk with his leather caning strap. 'You'll come to no good, Hope,' he'd shout. 'I can tell. You can see how a tree will grow by watching how the leaves blow, mark my words!' At the time I was worried. I wasn't sure what he meant, and most of the country seemed to agree with him on everything else. Maybe he was right. Even the weekly sermons in church condemned the pacifists who refused to fight the godless communists. But 20 years later I saw The Ox on a TV news item, being taken to court to face charges of sexual abuse of minors. So that's what my classmates were doing, I thought. That was the way The Ox's favourite leaves blew.

About this time the school entered a drama competition, and I got to play the Roman emperor in a school production of *Androcles and the Lion*. I was excited, it was my chance to shine. I had the best costume, a rich brocade curtain redesigned into an emperor's cloak. It was my voice, the headmaster said, that got me the part, my voice and my utter disdain for football. I looked much more like a decadent emperor than, say, a centurion, and there was no way I could be Androcles. He didn't explain why.

We travelled to Adelaide to present it. It didn't do well. One of the critics described my performance as having a 'Kenneth Williams camp approach'. This, combined with my occasional habit of reading at lunchtime rather than playing football or Red Rover, led to a rumour that I was a hermaphrodite. It was Westlands all over again. School life got tough for a few years after that. It put me off acting for a while.

Star Tour, Australia, spring 1994

I'm in a limousine on my way to meet Rolf and the publicist from Village Roadshow for a journalists' dinner and a day of interviews in preparation for the opening of *Bubby* in Australia. It's nine a.m. I'm fretting. I need to deliver my dole form to the city social security office. The publicist has arranged for the driver to take me there on the way to the meeting. I fear it may look a little ostentatious. When I signed on for social security benefits after Seattle, the woman taking my application frowned when she came to the 'usual occupation' section. 'Anything else?' she asked.

'How do you mean?' I replied.

'It says "Actor" here. Have you worked as anything else?'

'Well,' I said, 'I used to be a clerk for the post office, but that was more than ten years ago, before they brought in computers.'

She took her pen, and in the 'occupation' section, she wrote: Clerk.

There is a small queue that I have to run past at the dole office. 'I'm so sorry,' I say, 'the car, it's double-parked, I've got an interview.' People turn to look and see the silver limo outside. The driver casually waves. 'No hurry,' he shouts. I go bright red as I hand the form over. 'I can explain,' I say, and the social security officer nods. I run back out with everybody watching. The driver opens my door for me and I jump in. I wave apologetically at the sullen faces in the queue as the limo slides away. Then I sit back, reach into the drinks cabinet, and pour a glass of champagne. It comes with the car.

And it's a help. There's a feeling of triumph involved, sipping champagne in the back of a limousine at nine in the morning after a visit to social security. I can't wait to tell people; there's something about it that makes me feel real. A sense of importance. A sense of impending success, of waiting for the call from overseas, of enjoying the future in advance.

Rolf disagrees.

It's a moral thing. Every dollar spent on this comes out of the money that the film makes, he explains. Everyone who worked on the film is on points. Every dollar taken out of the profits is a dollar taken away from the points system. He implies that we have a responsibility; we owe it to everyone not to waste their money.

I squirm. I'm enjoying wasting their money.

There are some interviews, and then the luncheon. There are menus on the tables with my face all over them – the *Bad Boy Bubby* menu. Wow. The first journalists arrive and I'm introduced to them. I ask if they'd like a drink. I only have $20 left for the week, but I'm thinking that if I offer the first round, I'll get away with being bought drinks the rest of the time. Slow learner, I know, but here at least I know the prices, and if the journalists think I'm tight, they might write bad things. I'm on my way to the bar when Alan Finney, one of the heads of Village Roadshow Australia, stops me. 'Nicholas,' he says, 'the drinks are free.' I look nervously at Rolf, but he's already got one. This is obviously acceptable. 'Great!' I say.

There's a haze of alcohol, a stream of compliments. The

journalists love the film. They want to know where I've come from, where I've been hiding, how I got the role, how I did it so well, so convincingly, so accurately, intelligently, precisely, unaffectedly, genuinely, constantly . . .

The words ring and stick in my brain, I can taste them. I realise I *always* knew I was that good, I never *really* doubted my abilities . . .

'It was all in the script,' I tell the journalists humbly.

We've got two weeks of this. The *Bad Boy Bubby* Star Tour is going to Sydney, Melbourne, Adelaide and Brisbane. There's drinks all the way, and business-class plane seats, and limousines, free dinners, adoring journalists. All I have to do is be charming and humble. Wealth, I can see now, breeds relaxation and grace. I can feel my body taking on a more languorous air each day. It's a different world, and it's very desirable. I remember a quote I read in an article: Money can't buy happiness, money *is* happiness.

But we come cheap. One of our publicists talks of other, bigger stars who insisted on being supplied with models who double as prostitutes, at the distributors' expense. 'I had to ask for girls with specific measurements,' she says angrily. 'Then the next guy wanted to bring his wife, but asked that we give her a separate room for when we supplied his nightly escort. *And* he blamed us for not being allowed to carry his hand gun on the plane.'

I begin to think that Rolf is wrong, we're being very reasonable. I can feel my own guilty desire to request more. I don't know what, but maybe I'm selling myself short here.

There must be *something* I can think of that they could do for me. It's obvious I could make huge demands and they'd be catered for, the only reason I'm not is so that everyone'll like me. Maybe it's only the demanding people who are successful.

I tell Rolf the story of the prostitutes and casually mention that I think we are being quite restrained. He looks at me curiously and says, 'Nick, if you seriously want the services of a prostitute, all you have to do is pick up the phone.'

Damn. I can't tell if he doesn't understand, or if he just *chooses* not to understand.

In Sydney, the household I'm in is casually ignoring the fact that any interviews are taking place. They love the stories about big stars and prostitutes but glaze over if I get too excited about the free wine and food. I invite them and other friends to come and see a preview showing of the film. This, I know, will change everything. They won't be able to help but understand why I am so excited, why my life is about to change, just who this guy is they are living and hanging around with.

They stand in a group afterwards, not looking at me. 'It's homophobic,' says one. 'Sexist,' says another. 'Really good,' says a third. Then a university colleague approaches. 'Hmm,' he says. 'Rolf's a good director, isn't he?'

No one mentions me or my acting. I try to stay stoic, I understand, they must be jealous the selfish bastards. I close my eyes and think of Venice.

The next day there's a feature article in the *Sydney Morning Herald* that defines me as the 'man who will soon be famous'. There's a big photograph and lots of writing about how self-effacing I am about my huge talent. I leave the paper on the kitchen table, open at that page so my flat-mates will see it. I'm off to Melbourne – let them stew in their own envy!

Have you ever flown business class? And not paid for it? Most people who fly business class look like they don't pay for it. In business class you can stretch your legs out so they actually reach full length. You can make your seat go lower than in economy, so it's comfortable to sleep. The flight attendants take their time with you. You get champagne just because you're sitting on the aeroplane, and you get, or used to get, silver-plated knives and forks and great big cloth napkins and edible food. The wine is better quality, there's a bigger choice of spirits, the air is fresher, and you can stick your elbows out without hitting the person next to you. If you fly far enough, you can choose to watch R-rated films. It's how everybody should travel all the time. It's great. It's really great when you're on the dole and someone else is paying, and you know that once they've finished paying you'll be so famous that you probably won't ever fly less than business class ever again, and you'll never pay. You might even consider various compromises – maybe the odd Coke advert, or your face on a bank-loan brochure, or parts in movies you don't approve of – to make sure this happens. Who takes notice of adverts, you might reason, and who minds that film stars say yes to work? It's not compromise, it's just good sense. It's what anyone would do given half the chance!

Rolf, of course, disagrees. 'We should have flown economy,' he says. 'This is such a waste of money.'

'Maybe they want to make sure we're not too tired when we arrive,' I venture.

He looks pointedly at my third red wine. 'It's only a two-hour flight from Sydney to Melbourne,' he says.

My hotel room is to be used to hold interviews, so it isn't really a room. It's a suite as big as the house I live in in Glebe. The publicist, aware of Rolf's views on accrued expenses, nervously explains that it's important that journalists understand that the film is being treated very seriously by the company. *Bubby* is a difficult sell. Village are attempting to market it to a non-arthouse audience. The money spent on the release signifies the importance of the film.

I don't care, I'm only half listening, I'm squealing internally with delight. We have a couple of on-air interviews to do and I don't want to leave the room. The sheer expanse of it dizzies me. I'm only just holding back from checking what's in the bathroom, what's on the TV channels, what's in the bar fridge, how fluffy the dressing gown is. I want to hold on to it for as long as possible.

Our first radio interviewer hates the film. She finds the subject of incest aversive, the treatment of women questionable, the cinematic forgiveness of murder unpalatable. She attacks us both for being involved in it. We have a live-to-air shouting match. We scream over each other's voices. We call each other rednecks, idiots, moral reprobates (her to us), moral coward (us to her). I leave buzzing with adrenaline. This is Art!

That afternoon I'm still bouncing when I meet up with Alan Finney again. I've been thinking of the requirements other stars have had, I've been thinking of my own restraint, I've been thinking of Tromsø, and I've hatched a plan. I ask if there are any trainee positions in Village Roadshow. 'We do have them,' Alan says, 'but she'll need to have the right qualifications and speak good English.'

That night I ring Bianca from the hotel. I've already checked if I can. 'Sure,' said the publicist, 'just make sure you hang up. The last guy rang France when he was drunk and forgot to hang up and we had a $3000 bill in the morning.'

Bianca answers the phone in Norwegian. How exotic! I gush, 'If there were a job working in film to come to for a few months that ended up covering the costs, would you come over?'

'Yes,' she says.

I explain, 'There is a job, a traineeship. You just have to apply for it and a visa.'

Silence.

Then she says, 'I'll get on to it.'

It's already four months since we saw each other. My heart is pounding with excitement and fear. The memories are superb, erotic, electric. This could be good. But it's not Tromsø, it's not Rotterdam, it's not a catered festival. It could be terrible. It's a risk. It's the kind of risk I wouldn't, couldn't, have done before. That's the kind of person I am becoming.

I hang up carefully. King Nicholas arranging romance from the Arctic ice. Stuff you, social security 'occupation: Clerk' person. I'm an Actor. And I've got clout.

I go and meet the others for dinner. We drink too much, then go back to the suite to party and drink more. A homage to Tromsø. Before I pass out for the night, I realise that in inviting Bianca over, I neglected to mention the traffic noise, the share house, the dole, the cockroaches, the lack of festival comfort. I lie woozily on the king-size bed in my massive hotel suite, a social-security-registered unemployed clerk, surrounded by the detritus of a late-night party paid for by the publicity budget on my first film, and worry about the meeting of fantasy and reality.

When I get back to Sydney, the digital clock on the control panel of the microwave oven in the kitchen is obscured by cockroaches. There is a letter from social security asking me to attend a retraining session. There is a message from my agent: the last two auditions I attended were unsuccessful.

Sydney, spring 1994

The film's out and I'm waiting for the rewards. It's a long, long wait. I get stopped in the street a lot. People ask me to repeat lines from the film or sign autographs. They yell 'Hey Bubby!' or 'Hey Pop!' from passing cars. I get nominated for best actor in the upcoming Australian Film Industry Awards, against Hugo Weaving, Terence Stamp and John Hargreaves. I do stupid skits on TV chat shows and have more articles and photographs in gossip magazines. 'Balding Actor Makes Bad Boy Good' reads one set of headlines. But the film isn't a box-office success. I don't understand. Incest, grunge music, rape, sex, murder, exoneration – it's the kind of film I'd like to see. And the reviewers mostly love it. People who go to the cinema love it. I know, I sit in the back a lot. Audiences clap at the end of it. It's just hard getting people in.

Their loss, I decide. The Italians are bound to call soon and then I can leave this hicksville deadwater behind. Anyway, Bianca's on her way. The visa has been approved, my housemates have *agreed* to let her stay – as if they had a choice, who do they think they are, but I let it pass – and Bianca's family has loaned her the ticket money. It's remarkable how easy all this has been. She's happy to have the work, she's finished university, there are no jobs beckoning over there. Even if I turn out to be a dead loss she gets the beginning of a CV, or at least that's how I explain it. Secretly I'm surprised and impressed she's agreed to come. I don't think I'd have the guts to do what she's doing. Less than a week together in rarefied conditions eight months ago, and now a three-month stint in Cockroach House, Sydney. It might not be what she's expecting. I might not be what she's expecting. I'm already starting to suffer from performance anxiety and she hasn't even arrived.

When she does, I'm working. At last. A social worker on the ABC television series 'GP'. He's attracted to one of his younger charges, avoids the temptation of ravishing her and in so doing condemns her to a life on the streets. The irony doesn't escape me. But I'm getting paid $1000 for it, I'm rich again, I can entertain.

I'm able to pick Bianca up at the airport before going to the set. I hide behind a pillar, waiting for her to appear. I'm unsure if the same appeal will be there, whether the exoticism will be as apparent.

She's instantly recognisable. Tall, with a way of walking that makes her look like she's on stilts. She moves like a giraffe. Just before her feet are about to hit the ground they extend that little bit more, and the body sways with the movement. Her eyes have that curious oriental slant, her cheeks are flushed from the flight, her head floats on a slightly elongated neck. I can see all this from a distance, and I can see she has decided I'm not there, and it doesn't bother her. She's already striding towards the exit. I'm nervous as hell.

Tonight, Village Roadshow is holding a premiere for another film, *Priscilla, Queen of the Desert*, to which we are invited. This is good. I'm out working all day, then we'll go to a party at night. We don't have time to be awkward.

I've seen *Priscilla* before, in Seattle. It won the awards I wanted: best film, best actor. I remember how justifiably enraged I felt. On the bus ride into the cinema I apologise to Bianca for the film. 'There's a racist bit,' I explain, 'where a Thai woman who has been rescued from Thailand chooses to continue to do her Thai-prostitute act, shooting ping-pong balls from her vagina at a crowd of cheering Australian men, thereby emasculating her saviour husband.'

I pause, but there's no reaction.

'It's a big choice,' I continue, 'given that she is half the female cast of the film. Then there's a lot of bad jokes, and some picturesque Australian desert, and a bit at the end which tells us that homosexuals are normal people who are able to have children and aren't really any different at all. It won all these awards in Seattle, but then I know how awards are won there!' I add importantly, 'I don't think it will do very well.' She nods. She's jet-lagged.

I'm still lecturing her when we get there, all nerves and righteous babble. *Priscilla* has become the worst movie of all time by now, Bianca's lack of response spurring me on to greater and greater condemnations. There's a red carpet and hordes of photographers outside the cinema. Typical, I tell myself, the film's got Terence Stamp in it, Hugo Weaving's well known, Guy Pearce is big in television – they go all-out for a clumsy piece of offensive fluff just because it's got stars in it. Village didn't do this for *Bubby*!

We begin to walk down the carpet, and suddenly the cameras start flashing, and photographers start yelling, 'Nicholas! Look here! Nicholas! Nicholas!'

My ego soars. I grin from ear to ear. All at once I'm back in Venice. My posture improves. Bianca is in shock, she's blushing and staring at the ground. Phew! I think, this'll keep my reputation afloat.

Inside, Hugo Weaving comes up and tells me he's just been asked for an autograph by someone who thinks he's Bubby. I laugh good-naturedly. Hugo's being really nice. Should I tell him about the suit in Venice? Maybe not. I can't decide if it's funny or demeaning. Maybe I'm being a bit harsh on *Priscilla*. Then I'm approached by someone else who thinks I'm Hugo. This could be a problem. Hugo's a lot better known than me, he's taller and not bald. If people think we look alike, what chance have I got? There's a little panic building up. Photographers grab me and line me up for the social pages. Bianca's getting into the swing of it now, smiling at the cameras, holding hands. I soften my thoughts about Village, the panic starts to settle. Maybe *Bubby* didn't *need* a party!

I see Terence Stamp and I wilt. He's done early Ken Loach and worked with Pasolini. He looks like I would like to look at his age. He's standing alone in the cinema foyer, wearing a white linen suit that matches his hair. One of the Village publicists promises to introduce him. I try to plan what to say but don't come up with anything. We just shake hands and stare at each other. After a while he moves away.

The film's even more irritating the second time around. It carries the weight of Australian reputation on its back. Some part of what I represent is up there on screen and

Bianca is watching it. Worse still, the audience are enjoying it. They laugh at the Thais-are-all-prostitutes scene, coo at the homosexuals-as-mainstream-family cultural paradigm. My scalp prickles with mortification. I turn to justify them to Bianca, but it's okay, she's asleep. I don't have to excuse anything or even face the potential of her liking it. I wonder if I'm overreacting.

She wakes up for the party. It's huge. Drink, food, drag acts, bands, speeches. People in gowns and tuxedos. A ball room. Sydney masquerading as Europe. It's wonderful, it's everything I told her wouldn't happen here, it's as if I planned it specially for her first night. When she is intro-duced to Bill Hunter, who plays the husband of the Thai prostitute, she tells him she hadn't seen him in the film, she was too jet-lagged. He chooses to be charmed. In fact, I notice, most people choose to be charmed. She is charming. I stand in the middle of this major Sydney film premiere and watch her meeting her new employers, talking to journalists, gathering little crowds of admirers. I realise with a sense of pre-knowledge: Ah ha! She's an Asset!

Priscilla is the beginning. Bianca fits into Cockroach House as much as she fits into the Sydney social scene. My housemates adore her. They take her to gay clubs where she's mistaken for a drag queen. She's fearless, she's excited, she loves the trip to the Blue Mountains. She has photos of Norway, she gets phone calls from Britain, she thinks it'd be a good idea to visit my brother in Japan. She doesn't worry about money like I do. 'If it runs out we'll find something,' she says. 'Don't worry so much.'

I can't quite work out how we know each other so well. We're like a ready-made Celebrity Couple. Bianca and I might be living in a share-house slum, but we're getting invited to all sorts of parties. I'm the celebrity, she's the charmer. Everywhere we go the cameras flash, it's Sydney/ Venice and I'm in love with the world.

And no wonder. I can't do wrong. There are all sorts of parties happening. Screen directors' parties, Film Commission parties, Roadshow event parties, end-of-year parties for events or businesses that want celebrities like me to be present. Hell, I've been in *Who* magazine, crucified on a Hills hoist washing line. The photographer wanted me naked on the roof wrapped in gladwrap, to reflect Bubby, but I said no. I'd learnt something in Venice; I felt a religious image would be more fitting, more saintly. People see that stuff, and I'm an AFI nominee, I have to be careful. My photo is everywhere. Bianca and I have become social-page regulars, rent-a-celebrity-crowd members for the Sydney scene. If it weren't so exciting, it'd be embarrassing.

The AFI award ceremony is in Melbourne, and there's been a big build-up. All those social-page photos have been identified with tags like: 'AFI Award Hopeful Nicholas Hope with Bianca at . . .' or 'Bad Boy Hopes for Good Award!'. I'm very nervous. The AFI has flown me down and is putting me up in a hotel for the weekend. Bianca has been given time off from Village to attend. This is a big event. I've saved up enough money to spend $500 on a suit so

I don't have to wear another Hugo Weaving one. The irony no longer appeals. It takes ages to find one I like for that price, but someone in a Melbourne shop recognises me and digs up an out-of-date leftover from the storeroom.

There's drinks at Village Roadshow before the event. I'm so tense I down several. Then there's drinks provided by the AFI for invited guests, and since I'm presenting an award I go to those and drink some more. By the time everything starts I'm woozy, but the nerves aren't as bad. I sit with Bianca in the Melbourne Town Hall as the ceremony goes on and on. The awards are for television as well, there's a whole swag of them to get through for God's sake and there's a whole load of tacky Eurovision-style song and dance numbers in between each award. It's excruciating.

Then suddenly there's an interval and more drinks, and a lot more people floating around in identical suits, and women in backless dresses, and it starts to get exciting. People keep grabbing me and wishing me luck. 'Thanks,' I say, 'thanks.' An announcement is made, we're due back in, but I have to stay so I can present an award with Toni Collette, who's nominated for best actress. She's nervous, too, and we both get stuck into the wine, and she needs the loo but she hasn't got time to go before we've got to be on stage, and she's worried she might burst, and I have to read from the autocue, so I try to speed it up for her but I slur terribly and hear myself do it. My God, I think, the film community must see me as a confirmed alcoholic.

I go back to sit with Bianca, who says, 'You're drunk,' which I already know and can't see why she'd bother telling me, but it becomes irrelevant as *Bubby* starts to win all the major awards. Best editing: Suresh Ayyar, *Bad Boy Bubby*. Best script: Rolf de Heer, *Bad Boy Bubby*. Best actor: Nicholas Hope, *Bad Boy* – best actor? That's me! It's *my* name they're calling out and it's making up for Venice and the crowd is really excited, films like *Bubby* don't usually win these kinds of awards, I literally *run* on to stage. Someone has told us we only get 45 seconds to speak and that's really aggravating, all those crappy shopping-mall-entertainment routines have taken up *my* moment, but I try to think what to say and come up with the line: 'You've no idea just how gratifying this is!' and everyone laughs. I try to thank the right people and be intelligent through the haze of alcohol and pride, then go backstage and get photographed and interviewed and clapped on the back and photographed some more. Ha ha ha haaaa! I stagger round to re-enter the hall and take my seat, but there's someone in it. No one's told me that people are *employed* to fill the empty seats so the viewing public won't notice, and I don't want to cause a fuss, so I just go back to the drinks table and miss Rolf winning best director. I hear the crowd roar with approval.

There's a party afterwards, a huge event with food and drink and spaces I don't even get to see. Bianca tells me later that I missed the band and the dancing, there were several rooms I never got to, but hey, I don't care, I'm the Man of the Moment. I can't tell whether to be arrogant or humble. I want to be both but can't decide which one is going to bring the best results. I opt for pissed. I have conversations

I can't remember with people I don't know. At some time very early the next morning I am forced to shoo the last well-wishers out of our hotel room as they try to raid the mini-bar. Drunk or not, I'm not paying those prices for strangers – who do they think they are? I close the door on them in righteous victory.

Back in Sydney, I'm offered a role in the touring version of *That Eye the Sky*, a play directed by Richard Roxborough that will be happening early next year. Then I'm phoned by Paul Cox. He wants me to play one of the lead roles in his next film, *Lust and Revenge*, later in the year.

I've Arrived, and it's Good.

CHAPTER 5

stardom

The Jennings Estate, Whyalla, 1974

The Jennings Estate streets were cleaner. Most of them were cul-de-sacs, and the houses all had garages for the cars, and concrete driveways instead of loose shale. The gardens were landscaped. There were five different styles of bungalow on half-acre blocks. The rich migrants lived there.

Of course they did. It's where you'd want to be. It was where *I* wanted to be. I knew you couldn't ever aspire to being in the main part of town, because that's where the old families of Whyalla lived, the Aussies. They sort of owned the area. But this, this you could aim for. Bright, spanking-new houses with parents who bought you a little film camera so you could make movies with your friends. That's the kind of thing that happened in these houses. I knew, because I knew this girl, Gwendoline, who lived in one. That's what she did. Made little movies with her friends.

I liked visiting there. It was different. People spoke and ate differently. They had two forks and two knives, and meals with different courses. The house had a feeling of luxury, with all-new wallpaper and wall-to-wall carpet – incredible. And everyone looked good. I was enamoured of Gwendoline – enamoured seemed the correct word for it in that setting – who seemed to be responding to my attentions even though I was very awkward at showing them. She would stroke my hair playfully, invite me round to watch television at night. Her mum would say things like 'I'll leave you two alone then', which was a foreign idea in my world. None of the other parents I knew would say that, they'd be too scared of what might happen. So was I. Nothing did in the conventional sense, just long, raw moments of gaping embarrassment.

But it was enough to tell Sandra, the other girl who seemed to fancy me – the one I'd been able to meet after school and kiss, blowing into her mouth because that seemed to be what they did on TV and she didn't complain – it was enough to tell her it was over, I didn't think we were compatible. The truth was I liked her well enough. It's just that I'd met her parents, I'd gone round there one day for dinner. They wanted to meet this boy she was talking about. They were thin and worn-looking, they ate Smith's Crisps with dinner, they had the tele on while they ate. The furnishings were shabby, their faces mean and pinched. And their accents were all Strine, that peculiar nasal whine that comes with the more extreme Australian dialects. I couldn't take it, couldn't buy into it, couldn't keep blowing into Sandra's mouth in her friend's backyard caravan over the homework. It was far too threatening.

She cried out there on the oval of Stuart High School,

and I was sad for her, but it couldn't be helped and I could hardly go back now, could I? I stayed strong as I walked away and left her sitting there tearfully, and I didn't look back. I went to Gwendoline's house instead, and stood outside in an agony of indecision, but even that was better than the promise of Sandra's parents.

I stood there long enough for it to become dark, outside the Jennings house in the Jennings Estate, and listened to the frogs that started croaking in the little pools in the little landscaped gardens, and wished that my house was here and had little frogs. And then it struck me that they were all croaking in sequence, that you could time the croak. They were all recorded. They were fake frogs.

nicholas hope

Sydney, summer 1994

Bianca and I can't sit in the local pub any more because
people want autographs. They come over one by one from
the surrounding tables with napkins and pens, they sidle
out of the poker-machine gaming rooms with betting cards,
they buy us drinks and ask for Bubby impressions. I don't
know where they come from – not that many people have
seen the film, we know from the sales figures, but those that
have all seem to find me. We both get flown over to present
the South Australian Cinematographer Awards in Adelaide
and get put up in a suite of rooms in the middle of
Adelaide's red-light street. One of the organisers takes me
aside at dinner to tell me that I have a beautiful girlfriend
with great tits. I don't know if he's quoting a line from
Bubby, or being rude, or just horribly Australian. Sometimes it's hard to tell the difference.

In the dole office now I get treated with respect. The
woman who handles my case tells me I don't need to look for
alternative work, it's obvious I'm going to make it, not like
some of these other bludgers who call themselves actors, she
can tell. It must be the film or the award that has changed her
opinion of me, she never used to be so encouraging.

Marty rings from LA. He wants me to audition for some
new film called *Seven*. He wants to fax over the script, asks
if I have a fax machine. I need to read it, tape an audition,
and get it back to him in two days. The part is small, it's all
at the end of the movie, it's a serial killer, but I send the tape
off even though it costs a lot. Marty says the film might be
big, though it reads a bit low-budget to me.

It doesn't worry me that I don't hear back. It's all good and it's all exciting, but I'm wary after Venice and De Niro, I'm keeping calm. Bianca's three-month visa has run out so she's returning to Norway for Christmas. 'Come on over,' she says, 'you've got the frequent flyer points, try it out. You never know your luck, maybe something will happen over there. If it doesn't you can just come back. There's a few months before the play or the Paul Cox film starts. What else are you going to do?'

She makes it sound so easy, so accessible, so obvious. Then she adds, 'I'm visiting a friend in Los Angeles in January. You could join me on your way back here and catch up with that agent guy who keeps ringing.'

Oslo then Los Angeles. What could be more natural for a boy from Whyalla?

The North, winter 1994

Bianca has been busy. It's only been a week since she left Sydney and arrived in Norway, but she's already found out that *Bad Boy Bubby* is being released over Christmas. She's had a meeting with the Norwegian distributors, told them I'm coming over, arranged a Star Tour of Norway for me, with herself as publicist. She's excited – it's a coup and a holiday all in one, and it took some doing. She's exhibited daring and planning and initiative that is, frankly, scary. It doesn't fit the surreal family home we are in – a bright yellow Hansel and Gretel house in the middle of a forest on a mountain overlooking a fjord, her upstairs bedroom lined with childhood posters, her mother cooking a home-grown chicken downstairs in the kitchen that is decorated with now-banned articles from the family's colonial Indian past. I'm having trouble adjusting. This is a different fairytale from the one I thought I was in.

Bianca can sense my confusion. 'Relax,' she tells me. 'You're jet-lagged. Have a sleep, have some mulled wine, borrow some warm shoes and socks and clothes, and come for a walk in the forest white with snow. Don't think about the film until tomorrow.'

'Tomorrow?'

'Yup. We're meeting the distributors for dinner tomorrow.'

Dinner is at the company manager's house. Dark, gothic, heavy wood furniture. Gilt edges. Low lighting. The wife, the son, the daughter, lined up to be introduced. The wife's hands covered in rings, her neck smothered in necklaces. The son in his best designer suit, his hair bleached and quiffed in that Tin Tin style that seems so popular, like a smiling extra from *Cabaret*. The daughter in an expensive dress, looking sullenly at the ground. There are three other people here from the company. I am the only one of the four males present without a tie. My host pours me a glass of aquavit, a Norwegian national drink, and raises his glass. '*Skål!*' he shouts. It sounds like the Australian 'scull', and I swallow the drink in one as suggested. They look at me. 'It's good,' I say, 'tastes good.' They laugh and pour me another. '*Skål!*' says my host again, and I do. The others just sip, they're looking at me strangely. Am I getting something wrong here? They fill my glass again. Oh dear, it's strong stuff, I can feel it already. Bianca touches my arm, the model of decorum. '*Skål* is Norwegian for cheers,' she whispers. My host asks me how I like the country and adds, 'We have beautiful women, don't we?' I nod numbly and smile stupidly.

That's okay, he doesn't seem to expect much more. The company has business to attend to. There is a strategy to *Bubby*'s Norwegian release. The distributors are covered by a government policy that supports the release of limited-market films and provides a financial blanket to ensure that the public has a wide range of culturally diverse films to see. The film will start small, in a 40-seat cinema. They would like me to introduce it at its first screening on 26 December, Boxing Day.

He is looking at me, waiting for a response, a nod or a smile. I'm reassessing, feeling stupid. Limited market? They're already expecting to make a loss! Forty-seat cinema? Boxing Day? No one goes to the cinema on Boxing Day! I can sense embarrassment and disaster, introducing the film to the sad few sprinkled about a 40-seat cinema.

I'm trying my best to keep my thoughts to myself, and it must be working because now the distributors get down to detail and begin to explain the Star Tour. We will be travelling on economy trains and staying in small- to mid-range hotels to minimise costs. Damn. We will go to Bergen and Stavanger for one day each. Damn! We will have our expenses repaid when we return, so keep the receipts. Damn and double damn! We will do a couple of interviews here in Oslo before we go. The first one is early tomorrow, we should finish off dinner now and go home to sleep.

And that is that. They are beaming. I do my best to smile back. Where's the limousine? Where's the suite of rooms? Where's the business-class airfares? Where oh where are the per diems?

They tell me there's another film opening on Boxing Day, about the Lapps. Not very good but they will have reindeers in front of the cinema, and I'll get to meet them.

I can't wait.

They insist on taking a photo of me holding a horribly kitsch, evil-looking porcelain gnome that they call a Norwegian Nisse. When they give me a copy of the photo later, I can read the smile on my flushed face. It's the same as the one from my childhood at Alan-across-the-road's tenth birthday party. It was a celebration I didn't want to attend because I thought Alan too childish, but in recognition of his childishness I didn't want to hurt his feelings by not going. I, too, was ten, but I'd perfected the fake smile even then. It hasn't changed much.

The Oslo press conference is held in the corner of a large, cavernous, empty room above one of the cinemas. There's a collection of thermos flasks on the table, filled with a style of boiled, acrid coffee that seems to be standard here. The journalists have all taken a cup and the smell is sickly. The room is overheated and their coats, hung on hooks on the walls, are starting to steam as the snow caught in the pockets and on the sleeves and in the hoods starts to melt. The humid, wet-sock odour and the sullen, makeshift look reminds me of school camps.

They want to know why they should bother interviewing me, given they've already done it in Tromsø. Do I have anything different to say? Why have I bothered to come all this way to promote the film? Why come to winter when it's summer in Australia? Are they wasting their time, or is there a story here?

Bloody hell. I'm not prepared for this. I'm struggling and I'm not meant to be. They're supposed to like me.

'I'm here for love! I met someone in Tromsø, and I had to come back!' Flash! Flash! Flash! go the cameras. They want to know more: who she is, where she is, what she does. Bianca shakes her head. I mustn't expose her identity, my publicist shouldn't be my lover, that would be too gauche. 'I don't like to discuss my private life,' I say.

'In Norway,' says one of the journalists, 'we have some of the most beautiful women in the world, don't you think?' They wait, leaning forward, eager.

'Well,' I waver, 'I'm in love, so of course I think so.' Flash! go the cameras again. My stomach churns.

One of the women takes me aside. She is touched by my admission. If I'm to be here a while, she explains, I should know there is a Western being made by Nils Gaup, one of Norway's Oscar-nominated film directors. There could be a part for me. She says she knows the casting director. Maybe I could do an audition. She will give them a call if I'm interested.

The casting director rings the next day. I go in to audition the day after that. She videos us chatting. That's the audition. I will hear about the job after the Star Tour, she says. She's very hopeful. She thinks it's amazing I am here, and available. I agree. It's unbelievable.

The train chunts through a landscape totally foreign to me. Wide plateaus of ice-strewn landscape give way to harsh, jagged, glacial mountains. Fjords jut into the land. Islands are dotted off the coast, in a sea sluggish with cold. The sky is a swirling mass of angry purple clouds. Inside, the train drips with the wet from overcoats hung on hooks driven into the dark wooden panelling of the carriage. Bianca is loving it.

I am seething. The distributors are cheating us.

The law stipulates that we should both get per diems for the time we are away. To cover food and expenses. The distributors are making us use our per diems to pay for accommodation and transport, *as well as* food and expenses. They're stealing from us! Plus they've decided that Bianca doesn't qualify for per diems because she's my girlfriend, but they're asking her to do all the organisation, so they're swindling us twice over. 'It wasn't like this in Australia,' I explain, spitefully turning it into a national issue while attempting to doctor the receipts so we can get more back. Bianca doesn't let me. 'But they're using us!' I complain.

At least in Bergen they treat us well. Dinner, a tour, drinks, interviews, a quaint wooden hotel that the cinema people pay for. Once again I am asked if I find Norwegian women beautiful. It's becoming tiresome. 'It's a national obsession,' Bianca explains as I pose for photographs outside the line of bright wooden houses that border the harbour. 'Just ignore it.' I try, but when the cinema manager in Stavanger asks the same thing after forgetting we were coming and leaving us stranded and shivering at the railway station for over an hour, I can't. 'There seems to be a national obsession with the perceived beauty of Nordic genes that is a little disquieting,' I answer. 'Everyone here wants me to tell them how beautiful their women are!'

He looks at me. 'But they are!' he says with surprise.

When we get back to Oslo, I am all over the Norwegian papers. One of them even makes reference to my falling for a beautiful Norwegian woman. The distributors are ecstatic.

It's an amazing amount of publicity for such a small film, they explain, and we got it so cheap! They say that the distributors in Helsinki, Finland, have seen how much coverage we got and they want me to go there to do publicity as well!

Finland? I never thought I'd go to Finland. The timing fits perfectly with Bianca's departure to LA, and the Finns agree to pay per diems in advance, so it's like having a job. We arrange the flight to Helsinki to coincide with Bianca's flight to America. I will go on to visit my brother in London, then join her in the States, it's all so unreal. I ring the casting agent about the film, but everyone is on holiday. 'Don't worry,' she advises me.

Worry is my usual state, but everything else is working out so well, my picture is in all the papers, I'm in a curiously light-headed mode. 'Okay,' I agree.

It's Christmas Eve for me, Christmas for Norway. The air in the forest is cold and achingly fresh. Razor-edge walls of snowflakes balance precariously on the thin pine leaves of the trees. The sky is clear, but there aren't many stars visible. All around me the forest creaks, and there are constant *whooshes* as the build-up of snow is released and branches spring back into place. Then a soft, definite *thwump* as the snow hits the ground. An unplanned, untimed, percussive symphony. It is very foreign.

Inside the yellow Hansel and Gretel house overlooking the fjord, we sit with Bianca's family to eat a Norwegian delicacy spelt Pinnekjøtt but pronounced like the name of a Chilean dictator. Sheep's ribs dried out slowly over months, then rehydrated by steaming. An acquired taste. There is wine and aquavit. The family has dressed in Norwegian national dress. They sing Norwegian carols and dance around the table. We go to bed late. Tomorrow is my birthday. *Bubby* opens the day after.

The reindeer are smaller than I thought. They look painfully incongruous standing outside the packed cinema. There will be three sessions today, and all are sold out. I was wrong – everybody goes to the cinema on Boxing Day. The audience looks bemused that the Australian actor is here to introduce the film. One person asks why I'm not back in the sun. The 40-seat auditorium is depressingly small. There is one poster outside, from Australia, still with the creases from where it was folded to fit in an envelope. I am not convinced that the distributors are putting much effort into the release.

They take us as a special treat to Teaterkafeen, a restaurant opposite the National Theatre that has been there since the 1800s. It has bad caricatures of famous Norwegian actors, writers and artists all over the walls. The waiters are dressed in tuxedos. The food, when it comes, is overcooked and overpriced. I am surrounded by ties, hemmed in, claustrophobic. There is a building tantrum inside me that I can't place. Everything is promising and nothing is certain. How can this moment go unnoticed? I shouldn't be in this place, surrounded by these suits, crowded by formality and sunk in the morass of convention. I should be dining on caviar and champagne, I should be dancing on tables, I should be cavorting in ways I've never known, in lands I've never heard of.

One of the distributors leans over the table and interrupts my thoughts. 'Nicholas,' he says, 'have you ever been to Helsinki before?'

Helsinki, winter 1994/95

The matt-black curtains of the hotel room brush the walls. The window arcs slightly between them. It produces an optical illusion, an impression that the window is the entire wall, though it isn't. Outside, a light mist is settling in, and the fog lamps are starting to glow orange. A tanker is slowly pressing its way across the view, creating waves on the calm sea that ripple out to the moored rowboats just offshore. It keeps hooting mournfully on its foghorn. Along the harbour frontage a market is packing up, but some late shoppers are still buying. There are a lot of little fishing vessels with the crew selling the day's catch, and there are craft stalls mixed in with stalls selling trashy tourist trinkets. Everything is dim, the light appears stolen. I could watch this for hours.

I have just returned from the Finnish press conference and am in a reflective mood. Helsinki is a Gothic-looking city. Black and white. Piercings, leather, heavy make-up and cold, dim light, the set of a James Bond movie. Being here alone, in my room overlooking the harbour and the Baltic Sea, my brain has clicked into slow motion. I can hear how my shoes will crack through the thin film of snow on the ground and see how my beret will be out of place in a world of ear muffs and hooded coats. I can see myself walking through the frozen streets looking slightly discrepant but also partly assimilated, a foreigner but not an alien.

It is a comforting impression. I know my picture will be in tomorrow's papers. People here will read about me, see me in tomorrow's streets, go to see me on the cinema screen. They will develop fleeting thoughts based on articles about me, accompanied by photographs next to reviews of the film about a deranged innocent that I appear in. They may recognise me in tomorrow's coffee shops, and smile or shy away or try to talk. I am soon to be a part of the city, on the verge of recognition and acceptance in a part of the world I had never before considered.

There's just one problem. I'm having trouble controlling the image I want to portray. I've done the interviews. The journalists here want me to be psychotically deranged. They've been reading about Daniel Day-Lewis, they understand how Method acting works, they know I couldn't do the role without having lived the life for at least three months. One of them used to be a psychologist, he said the portrayal was disturbingly close to a disturbed person – how did I manage to get there? Did I spend time in the room, living and sleeping? Did I spend months in preparation?

'No no,' I said. 'Well, yes, I did prepare, but it was more reading than anything else, and crawling on the floor a bit like a cat, I mean it's all in the script, if you understand it then you can act it.'

'Ahhhh,' said the ex-psychologist, 'so you had no problems understanding it . . .'

'Well,' I replied in exasperation, 'you *saw* it and had no problems understanding it!'

'Yes, but I'm *trained* to recognise it,' he answered.

They wanted to know my life story. They were only satisfied when Whyalla came up, and the Catholic Brothers' all-boys' school. Finally, the film made sense. The photographer, who had been listening in, took me into the court-yard and leant me against some rusted iron railings in front of a broken, dripping drainpipe that was loosely attached to a peeling brick wall, then asked me to crouch down. 'It will look feral,' he explained, 'deranged and imprisoned, like you. Your character.' I nodded and smiled. 'No!' he shouted. 'Don't smile! That's not right. You don't smile!'

Once we'd concluded the press conference, I mentioned the problem to Mika, the Finnish distributor. Mika was different from the Norwegians. He was dressed in a shaggy fur coat and had a purple and green spectacle chain and long, curly hair. I felt I could talk to him, he was rock'n'roll. I told him that they were trying to manipulate my image, that I was worried about it. Mika shrugged. 'It doesn't matter,' he said, 'now we party.'

He's waiting downstairs now, as the tanker crosses the window. I have to get ready. We're meeting up with friends of Mika's from Germany, then we're going to his flat to eat takeaway elk hamburgers, then we're starting the night at a specialist vodka pub owned by one of the Kaurismaki film director brothers. The tanker in the harbour hoots again. This, I think, is what the outskirts of the world should be like.

The evening is so much vodka it gets late, and my hotel locks its doors and it takes me an hour to wake the porter and get in. I sleep until it's time for the plane to London so no one has the chance of recognising me in the streets or coffee shops. My photo is in the paper all right, looking grim and menacing and unsmiling by the rusty railings with the dripping pipe behind. I can't read the article because it's in Finnish, and I can only guess what the caption beneath the picture says. Mika seems happy. We drive out of the city past a naked man standing on a busy corner talking to an old woman. Nobody seems to notice that he is naked, that the temperature is below freezing. The man himself looks quite relaxed. I point him out to Mika, who nods. 'Must be cold,' he comments, but he's more interested in pointing out the various buildings. I wonder whether the man is homeless or disturbed or had too much vodka last night. Or if he's just being Finnish.

Los Angeles, winter 1995

I keep getting lost. Marty has told me how to find his office, but all the streets are named after numbers and compass directions. There's no public transport to speak of, taxis don't seem to exist, and I've had to hire a car for the first time in my life. It's being paid for by credit card and the financial worry is already making me nauseous. And Americans drive on the wrong side of the road and sit on the wrong side of the car. The city is huge and sprawling with no landmarks, the mountains can't be seen for smog, the roads go on indefinitely, and you can only tell you've changed suburbs by the number of Hispanics on the street. I keep expecting to be carjacked, but I smile at them anyway because I know this is a racist attitude, yet when I finally stop to ask directions it is a white Caucasian male I approach. Just chance, I tell myself, just chance.

Marty has organised a series of meetings with the department heads at all the major studios. He argues that since I'm a no-name actor over 25 years old, in Hollywood terms no casting agent worth their name is going to take the risk of suggesting me for a role. So I'm going straight to the top and seeing the people who make the real decisions. I get the list, but I don't know who they are or what these people represent, and I'm not sure what I'm going to say. 'Just chat to them,' Marty advises. 'They've all seen *Bad Boy Bubby*, they're keen to meet the actor who did the role.'

I'm a travelling freak show.

First there's a slinky middle-aged woman at the Dino De Laurentiis studio who looks like she's walked straight out of the 1950s. Dressed in a flowing silk gown and reclining on a chaise longue, she asks me to stand in the middle of the room so she can see me. She looks me up and down, then motions me to sit. 'What would you like to know?' she asks. I want to know if she can get me in a big-budget film, but it doesn't seem the right thing to say. Besides, I thought *she* wanted to know about *me*, wasn't that the idea?

Next there's a man at Paramount who loves the film *Bubby* but can't see how anyone in America could possibly release it.

Then at New Line I'm told how well Guy Pearce came across during *his* meeting. I get invited to the monthly Dreamworks staff party, but it's going to be on the day I leave. A woman at Warners tells me that she's just come from a development meeting where the only decision made by the all-bar-one male board is that for their next film they will cast Winona Ryder, 'and this time we'll get to see her tits!'. In another studio lot somewhere, in another numbered building that the guards direct me to, some minor development executive proudly tells me that we'll get on because he likes Art films, and he's currently developing a remake of a Krzysztof Kieslowski film, it's just taking a while because he hasn't decided which one.

I'm starting to doubt Marty's tactics. These people like meeting me, but there's no talk of employment. And as the meetings progress, there's some very shonky-looking studios in run-down areas of town, with schlock-horror posters on the walls, drawings of women screaming while a knife in the corner drips blood on to their heads and semi-exposed bosoms. A lot of the staff don't seem sure why they are meeting me. We have awkward conversations about accents and intercontinental distances and visas and box-office clout. They ask questions about Marty. Who is he? How did we meet? Are there any other actors on his books? Why aren't I with William Morris or someone? Do I know Mel Gibson?

In one meeting a mute secretary leads me into a large office where a man is sitting behind a desk. He immediately stands and strides across the room, talking as he comes to meet me, cutting across my own faltering introduction, hand outstretched. 'Nicholas,' he says, 'so pleased to meet you! I've heard so much about you! Your performance was breathtaking!' He meets me in the middle of the room, takes my hand in his, puts his arm across my shoulders, swivels me round, moves towards the door still talking. 'When's the film getting released here? You *must* invite me to the premiere! Here's my card.' He puts it in my pocket, opens the office door. 'Anything you need while you're here, and I mean *anything*, just call me, my home number is on there!' As he gently, firmly pushes me out he continues, 'It has been *such* a pleasure meeting you, I've heard *so* much about you! Have a nice day!' and shuts the door.

An 'insurance meeting', Marty calls it when I question why. In case I get big, the guy has met me and offered help. Happens all the time. It's a good sign. We just need that extra step where people put me in something that's big, so my name will be seen as being attached to money-making projects. Not arty ones. Art: good for respect, death to career.

If you wanna work in this town you gotta get away from Art and fast. Marty rings around, looking for auditions. There's a project about to enter pre-production, with Robert Redford and Jodie Foster attached. It's about the Ebola virus, and it's racing another project about the Ebola virus with Dustin Hoffman attached. Marty knows that Jodie Foster has probably seen me act because she's preparing for a film called *Nell* and her office requested a screening of *Bubby* for research, so he rings the casting agent for Jodie Foster's Ebola film.

The casting agent isn't interested. Marty shouts into the phone, 'What? Who the fuck do you think you are? You realise what you're missing out on here? This is the next Gary Oldman! Don't tell me I didn't warn you! . . . Well, screw you, too!' He puts the phone down. 'Just give them a minute,' he says. The phone rings. Marty picks up. 'Certainly, sir,' he says sweetly. 'What time? Can you fax over the sides?'

'What are sides?' I ask.

'The words,' he says. 'You know, the pages, the sides.' Bloody hell, I think, why can't they speak English?

The audition is in an hour, at the studio. 'They don't want to run the risk of missing out on the next Gary Oldman,' says Marty.

'That's a big call,' I answer.

The casting agency is in a caravan on the studio block. It looks temporary. 'So you're the next Gary Oldman,' says the agent when I introduce myself. This is a reasonable role, he tells me, which they would like played with an English accent. My part is a dithery professor type who is studying the Ebola virus and will be the first to die from it. 'But,' he adds, 'you get a scene with Robert Redford. This is that scene. Have you read it?'

I've read it. Hell, I've learnt it. I get to tell Robert that the monkeys in the laboratory have Ebola. There's not much more to it than that, it's straight exposition. A dithery English man in a sealed laboratory with Robert Redford speaking to him through a circular window in the door. I can guess who the camera would favour.

Another man enters the caravan. 'This is Max,' the agent says, 'the reader. He'll read Robert's part.'

'Hi,' I say, holding out my hand, 'I'm Nicholas.' Max takes my hand and says the first line of the scene. I recognise it. He's starting the audition straight away. I'm thrown, but I don't have the courage to stop him and request that we start again. We do the first few lines of dialogue still with hands held from the handshake. It's my first Hollywood audition. It's ridiculous.

I wonder if this is ordinary or if they're getting back at me for not being Gary Oldman. I'll never know. Marty has arranged another audition, for something called *Heat*. The scene only has three lines, but Marty thinks it's worth it. I'm not so sure, the guy dies at the end of the scene, he's basically a talking extra. But I go. 'It's important this casting agent sees you,' says Marty. 'There are no small parts, just small actors.' Yeah yeah, sure.

The agent seems utterly surprised that I know my three lines. She keeps saying, 'You know your sides, wow!'

'There aren't many to know,' I reply.

'Yeah, but you *know* them,' she says again. 'Wow!' Then she turns to the man beside her. 'Doesn't quite look right, does he?' she says.

'No,' he replies. It's as if I'm not there.

They turn back to me. 'Thanks for coming,' they say, 'and thanks for learning your sides. That was so impressive.'

I want to know why I'm not being sent to real castings. Three-line parts or a scene through a porthole before dying aren't what I had in mind when I thought of Hollywood. Guy Pearce is being considered for a lead, the New Line woman told me so, and he was in 'Neighbours', for heaven's sake! I was in a film that won awards in Venice! I won an AFI award for best actor in Australia! Doesn't that count for anything?

It does. Norway has called. They want me to play the sheriff in the film I auditioned for over there. James Caan and Christopher Lambert are the stars. I have to grow a beard and learn how to ride a horse. They want me for 12 days, spread over three months. Shit. It's a role in a Hollywood film. With Hollywood stars. It could be the beginning of something big. And I'd get to stay with Bianca. But while the amount they are offering is reasonable, it's not enough to live on for three months and they're not going to put me up.

I can't afford to do it. I have to say no! I can't believe it. Neither can Bianca. Neither can Marty.

The Norwegians double the offer.

So here I am, sitting in Marty's office with the offer of a part in my first Hollywood film. The money's not bad. I'll learn to ride a horse. I'll be in a Western. I'll get to stay with Bianca. The next three months are covered. It's relaxing, energising. And now the phones are ringing with other sideline follow-through offers. Dinner with the people Bianca has been visiting, who are making a film that she has helped out on. Dinner with the man from Paramount and the woman from Warners. Dinner with a director I met in Seattle whose flat we've been staying in. All this free food to be had and then a job; Marty's tactics must have worked. There are just a few things to be cleared up with the contract, and a little item to be dealt with back in Australia – that dry colony where I used to live, somewhere in the Southern Hemisphere.

I ring my agent there, to tell him I have accepted a Hollywood film offer and am therefore no longer available to do the country tour of the play I've already committed to doing. I am surprised he's not thrilled. He's angry, and unkindly terse. 'They've already done the publicity brochures with your name and photo on them,' he states. 'They could sue you. They have every right to sue you. This is not an honourable thing to do. Are you sure you want to go ahead with it?'

I pause. What is there to say? Marty looks over at me. 'Why would you want to do a play?' he asks.

We are at dinner with the people Bianca has been helping. They have been making a film they all hate about death and orgasm. They are sitting around the producer's table in a sizeable house with an expansive back garden, complaining about the financial necessity of making such crap films when everyone knows they won't get a release. They remember working on better films, with Bob and Marty. They share stories about Bob and Marty, and Sharon in the latest one. Everyone nods: they know these people, we don't. Marty is a stickler for detail, and Bob, woah, Bob! What a character! And did you know Sharon got so upset on this last one that Marty spent so much time with Bob she complained, and Marty was so good he started spending time with her, too. That's the kind of guy he is, generous, generous and detailed. I ask who Bob and Marty and Sharon are. It's De Niro, Scorsese, Stone, didn't you know? I understand. It's a hierarchy. You have to be on the ladder. I am. Soon I'll be able to talk about Jimmy and Chris, and Nilsy the director. I'm on my way.

The man from Paramount and the woman from Warners know each other, and they've decided to do a joint restaurant treat shared between their monthly expense allowances. It'll be a restaurant to be seen in, they explain, an LA experience. I'm flattered. The meetings must have been worthwhile. I have made a tiny dent in Hollywood, the beginnings of a climb to stardom. And now I've got a Hollywood role I'm 'in the loop', as they say. I *need* to be seen.

It's a full table: Mr Paramount and his Russian wife; Ms Warner and her partner; myself and Bianca. And another aspiring actor who sits next to me, bouncing puppy-like in his chair. A friend of Mr Paramount. I don't understand why he's here. He takes over straight away with a story about his last audition: how well it went, who else was there, what he thinks his chances are. The story is all fragmented – he's too excited, people stop listening. I'm embarrassed for him but also pissed off. He's ruining my night.

He finishes and looks round for a response. Ms Russia rubs her husband's leg seductively and says, 'Can we have Beluga? I just love the Beluga here!' It's not what Mr Actor was looking for. I know the signs – he laughs too loudly and shouts, 'It's a speciality, the Beluga here is a speciality!' Mr Paramount looks at his wife and rubs her leg back. He looks across at Ms Warner. 'How much can your expense account take?' he asks.

The Beluga is $250 a serve. Ms Russia exclaims that she will eat a lot of it, she can't help herself, it's her ancestry, we need at least two serves. I wonder if we will have anything other than caviar to eat, and whether Bianca and I should just leave now. Petulance is rising in my throat as I watch the hijacking of a dinner I thought was in my honour. Mr Paramount turns dotingly to his wife and tells her she can order the Beluga, that's okay. Ms Russia rubs his leg again. When the caviar arrives, Ms Russia is right. You don't get much for $250, or even for $500. She could eat the lot by herself. She does.

When our hosts call for 'the check', the waiter arrives with a folder under his arm. I suspect it is a classy way of presenting the bill. I'm wrong. He hands the account to Mr Paramount, then lays the folder open on the table. 'I really respect what you are doing at Paramount, sir, and just want to give you this for your consideration.' Ms Russia giggles, no one else does. 'Thank you,' says Mr Paramount, and the waiter disappears.

It's headshots and a CV. I remember the girl in Venice. I wonder whether the waiter is jealous of Mr Paramount's guests. Does he think we are that much further up the acting ladder than he is? Are we? Is he embarrassed at what he did? Does he think it will work? Who does he think I am? Is he impressed that Mr Paramount is taking me to dinner in this restaurant? What would he think if he knew I have a Hollywood feature film coming up with Oscar-winner James Caan in it?

God, it's gratifying.

The next night, Brad, the director I met in Seattle, takes us to his favourite Chinese eatery in downtown LA. We're the only people there. It's not a place to be seen. 'It's authentic LA,' Brad tells us. 'I wanted you to see the real city.' There's machine-gun fire in the streets nearby; helicopters fly overhead trying to spotlight the people with the machine guns. Brad and his spindle-thin, hyperactive girlfriend are unfazed. Bianca and I are having trouble eating, the guns sound awfully close. 'Not a problem,' says Brad. 'The owners have probably got firepower.'

After the meal, they drive us into the Hollywood hills.

The whole of Los Angeles spreads out towards the horizon in the dark. Lights glitter like a star field. The hum of the city is an amplification of conversations and television in nearby houses mixed with traffic noise, sirens, gunshots and electronic buzz. An amalgam of urban noise and light from a metropolis almost totally devoted to the creation and consumption of visual entertainment. It is so attractive.

Marty is concluding the deal with the Norwegians. There is a fight over where my name will appear in the credits. I'm more concerned with the bit that says I won't be paid for rehearsals or for days I'm called but not required. 'They should pay for my time,' I say, but Marty just wants me to have a major 'above the line' credit on my CV. If my name isn't in those first credits then I may as well not do the film as far as he's concerned, because I'm not in it as far as Hollywood's concerned.

I'm more worried about surviving for three months. That clause that they can call me to work but don't have to pay if they don't use me is a bit of a worry. It sounds illegal. What if they simply don't pay? And there's my Australian agent, who has rung to tell me that the play I was supposed to be in has recast, has redone all the brochures, has agreed not to charge me for the cost. I can't bring myself to tell him about the dodgy contract. What if he asks about the credits, or tells me I'm stupid, or says it's not worth it? 'Thank them for me,' I tell him lamely.

'This film,' he answers, 'had better be good.'

CHAPTER 6

being
nike hope

The Bank, Adelaide, 1975

It was 110 degrees Fahrenheit and Spencer Street was a
mirage. I sweltered. The bitumen, the corrugated-iron
roofs, the tin-can cars sweltered with me, melting hazy
images into the fog of heat. If you let your mind wander
you could pretend you were somewhere else, that you were
walking through water and that was the reason your shirt
stuck to your skin and your shoes were like puddles.

I was walking in slow motion up and down Spencer
Street, trying to find a Verbal Agreement Form. Jerry from
the bank had sent me out to the post office for one. If they
didn't have it then I had to try the newsagent, then the
council, then the other three banks, and so on. I wasn't to
come back without one. I knew there was no such form,
that Jerry was trying to make a fool of me, but I didn't
much care. It was good to be out of the bank. I'd look for
hours if I had to, anything to avoid work. I wasn't sure why

I was there. It'd seemed a good idea to leave school and this was the first job, the only job, I'd gone for, because there was a sign outside saying they needed bank clerks. I'd never dreamt of being a bank clerk. I had no answers to any of the questions in the interview. The polaroid they took of me showed a surly, badly dressed 16-year-old scowling at the camera. But I was the only male applicant, the manager told me so, and the girls were likely to get pregnant, so I got the job. I hated it, but everyone said maybe if I worked hard it'd get better, the job had prospects and perks. Cheap home loans, study leave, promotional opportunities, security, superannuation. Things you shouldn't pass up, and jobs were getting scarce. I was a lucky boy.

The Alucards were already gathering outside the Spencer Hotel so I crossed to the other side of the road. Hannah, one of the bank's machinists – blonde hair, chubby arms, big breasts – was married to their leader, but that didn't guarantee security. They named themselves after Dracula, spelling the name backwards, but Alucard sounded singular so they had to add an 's'. I wondered privately about the comic Goth quality of naming a bikie gang after Dracula, whether they were being intentionally self-deprecating, but I doubted it. They seemed to take themselves very seriously. The whole of Whyalla took itself seriously. I stayed on my side of the road.

No one had a Verbal Agreement Form, but everyone pretended they existed. I understood. It was one of those initiation activities, a gentle form of having your head stuck down a toilet or your genitals mutilated, something meant to hurt or humiliate in order to make you an adult. I knew it was something I had to endure, that eventually the games would cease and I would be accepted. At least I wasn't being hit. But there was a worry. The adult world I was being initiated into wasn't what I thought it might be. I'd thought it would be an advance on school, that the world after initiation would release the secrets of desire and knowledge and power and satisfaction. But it didn't look that way. It was just a bigger, clumsier, less supervised continuation of school, and the people in it were pumped-up versions of the classroom in different uniforms.

I sat in a café drinking a milkshake. I reckoned I could stay away from work at least another hour before going back to report on the lack of Verbal Agreement Forms and facing the ridicule I knew would come. I watched the flies winging heavily through the heat haze over the Balfours white sandwich bread and the rolls of Fritz pressed meat. Above my head hundreds more flies were buzzing helplessly, stuck to a flystrip swinging in the air current. I sympathised. They were being punished, just for doing what was expected.

I had tried. I'd joined the basketball team and the Jaycees and tried tae kwon do. I'd gone to the staff Christmas dinner and watched second machinist Wanita's boyfriend trying to flirt with Sofia the clerk, watched the tellers Jerry and Paul and Jon try to flirt with Wanita, watched Wanita flirt back. I'd watched Mr Lowby, the Pommie accountant, stand and shout 'hear hear' when the comedian told the woman who complained about the sexist jokes to go get a sense of humour. I'd seen Jerry stagger to the toilet and his fiancée shout at Wanita and Wanita's boyfriend vomit under the table. It wasn't my vision of a life worth living, but I didn't have an alternative in my head and everyone seemed to expect it of me. If I just tried hard enough maybe I'd get used to it. Okay, so it wasn't my choice, I'd sort of wandered into it, but it was a job with a future, it was a grown-up thing.

The Whitlam Labor Government was sacked by the governor-general that year. There were rumours the CIA was involved. Everything went topsy-turvy, the whole country was turned emotionally upside down. Promised national strikes were called off at the last minute, mass indignation fizzled to nothing. It gave me a chance to be radical. A moment of confusion to change my life. I left the bank.

Rjukan, winter 1995

At seven a.m. a mini-van pulls up outside Bianca's yellow
house to take me to rehearsals. The passengers are concerned that I have no luggage; we are going to be away for
two weeks. 'Two weeks?' I say. 'I thought it was just a day!'
They look bemused.

'Rjukan is a five-hour drive from here,' they say.

'Rjukan?' says Bianca. 'You're going to Rjukan?'

'I'll just pack,' I reply.

Inside, I thrust things into a suitcase. Bianca helps,
adding folded scarves and jumpers and windproof jackets.
'Rjukan is so beautiful,' she explains, 'but it will be freezing.
You need warm clothing, you should have told me.'

'I didn't know,' I snap. 'No one told me!'

I'll be rehearsing for a week unpaid before I start
working on the film. I've already spent four intensive,
painful and frightening unpaid days learning to ride a horse
in the snow. The $2000 I brought over has gone. I'm
dependent on the first day's pay, and I don't know when it's
coming. And now this! Why didn't anyone mention the
two weeks away? How come no one mentioned the week's
rehearsal and first week's shoot were on location? How was
I supposed to know where Rjukan was? Bloody Norway!
First it steals my publicity per diems, then it steals my
rightful pay, and it doesn't explain anything properly!
I mumble a surly goodbye to Bianca as the car drives off.
Some of it has to be her fault.

A man called Mikkel sits in the front seat. As we drive
away, he begins to sing in a kind of mesmeric yodel. It's a

traditional Sami song style called a '*joik*', I am told, and Mikkel is a native Sami, they *joik* all the time. He maintains it for the full five hours. Øyvind, who sits beside me on the back seat, turns after the first hour and asks, 'How does it stand with you?' A third actor sits on the other side and lights up a cigarette which blows back in my face. It's too cold to open the windows so the car slowly fills with smoke. I cough but no one gets the hint. Outside, the view has turned into valleys of ice with stark, leafless trees silently piercing the white. There are sudden glimpses of unfrozen water from the fjords, and ice-skaters gliding across frozen lakes. The sky is a pale blue, the road a single black vein beneath it. The sun glitters on the snow. It's so bright I have to wear sunglasses. Everything is foreign. Øyvind wants to know how much I am getting paid. Everyone, he tells me, is angry at the conditions – unpaid rehearsals, minimum wages – but they all want to work with this director. I tell him how much I am getting and he goes silent. For the rest of the trip we just have the engine noise and Mikkel's *joik*.

We arrive in time for dinner. Rjukan, it seems, is the name of an area, not a town. There is a huge, barn-like lodge sitting on top of a hill, surrounded by other hills. This is where we are staying. It's designed for serious cross-country skiers. The facilities are basic, an upmarket youth hostel. The ceiling of my room sits a foot or so above my head. Its single fluorescent light flickers epileptically. Dinner is down the hall, in the common dining room. Fish and two vegetables, all prepared in the massive kitchen to the side, all overcooked. It comes with water, stewed tea, or a Norwegian version of Caterers Blend instant coffee. It's sparking faint memories of Mancunian school cafeterias: mashed potato fights, the smell of wet woollen socks, the constant threat of nausea. It's not my vision of working on a Hollywood film.

There's a production office down another hallway where people are queuing up to collect their per diems so they can go to the bar. When it's my turn, the line producer looks at two lists of names. 'So, you are not on a special rate!' she says, putting down the first list and picking up the second. 'What?' I ask. I can feel disaster lurking. 'The foreign actors, they normally get a special rate, but not you. See?' She points to the list of names – Beatte, Bjørn, Mikkel, Nicholas, Nils, Øyvind, Ragnar. 'You are on the Norwegian rate.'

'How come?' I ask. 'I'm not Norwegian!'

'You are for now,' she answers. 'You must have been hired from here.' It clicks. That's why they're not putting me up in Oslo, that's how they've got away with not paying per diems in between shooting dates, that's why Marty's having a hard time with the credit. They're pretending I'm Norwegian for budget purposes. Bloody Norway! She hands me 40 kroner. 'That's it?' I say. It's less than the price of a beer.

'Yes!' she says. 'It is enough!'

'Could I have the full two weeks at once, then?' I ask.

'No! No special favours!' she replies. 'Next!'

Something is wrong here. Marty has ushered me into the land of Calvinism. How come I'm not on a special rate? What's wrong with me? Who worked this out? How am

I going to survive? What does it say about my status? Is it important? Do I accept Øyvind's offer of a beer, and wait until tomorrow to buy him one? Do I refuse, and look anti-social? Do I admit I have no money other than the 40 kroner? He already knows what I'm getting paid, it won't ring true. I'm developing a headache.

We rehearse the first week. Horse riding in the mountains, stunt training in the snow. My horse keeps tripping over its own feet and catapulting me over its head. I develop a twitch every time it staggers forward, and when the others gallop off with enthusiasm and my horse tries to follow, I grip the saddle with both hands in an attempt to stay on. My sheriff is a wuss.

The stunts are easier. Hitting, being hit, getting shot – I'm a natural at reacting to pain, real or fake. The stunt coordinator praises me and starts to use me to demonstrate the stunts. 'You could be a professional stuntman!' he says, loudly. My co-actors murmur with respect. They ask me to show things again. I swell with pride. My bearskin coat costume makes the falls painless. I begin to enjoy myself. This is more exotic than country Australia.

Then the stars – James Caan and Christopher Lambert – arrive. The press gets flown up to photograph the two of them posing in motorised ski cars, and huge luxury caravans get parked outside to house them. Lambert brings a posse of models with him, and another office gets set up for the cluster of assistants and personal chefs. My excitement fights uneasily with my jealousy. At least this is Hollywood, I tell myself, but Bianca puts me right. She wants me to be accurate about what I am doing. 'You are not in a Hollywood film,' she tells me over the phone. 'You are in a European co-production with Hollywood stars. It is different.'

I'm still excited. The potential seems big, and beautiful. I know now I've made the right decision – how could I have made any other? I'm being paid to have an experience! On my days off, I go for walks in the surrounding countryside, stepping in the ski tracks left in the snow by early morning skiers. There are miniature frozen waterfalls hanging off rocks, whole valleys of snow-white pine trees. At one point a flock of birds seems to rise up out of the snow in front of me and flap off as one, snowflakes scattering from their wings as they fly. When I ring Bianca to tell her, she is more concerned about the ski tracks. 'Tourist!' she says. 'Don't step in the ski tracks. The skiers need them. *Herregud*! How can you be so Australian!'

There is a growing racial tension as the film gets closer to the beginning of the shoot, a reflection of its co-production origins. The French head the costume department. The Norwegians grumble that the French have no concept of the cold. The English distrust the French, who in turn look down on the English. The Americans doctor the script in an attempt to make it more commercial. The Hollywood script doctor tells us all what improvements he has made. 'At least now,' he sneers, 'the bad guy gets killed and the good guy gets the girl!' The actors complain that the only things that made the script interesting have disappeared.

On the first day of shooting there is a riot. The Norwegians are in charge of catering. It is minus 20 degrees Celsius, and lunch is a thin stew plus some slices of bread with cheese and ham on top. The French are outraged. They gather in a group at the entrance to the meal tent, slamming their plates on tables and pouring the stew contemptuously into the snow. 'This is not fuud!' they shout, and threaten to stop work.

The Norwegians don't understand. This is what they generally eat for lunch. If it's good enough for them it's good enough for everybody, who do these food snobs think they are? The English agree with the French, but don't want to be seen supporting them. The Americans have all flown in their own food anyway, so they don't notice. I'm with the French; we need decent food to eat. Besides, the Norwegians were right about the costumes: we actors are freezing out there. We need something to warm us up.

A compromise is found; something will be done about the situation tomorrow. The set divides into its constituent languages. The Norwegians grumble about the French in Norwegian, the French about the Norwegians in French, the English about everybody in English.

I don't grumble. I'm excited. Things are getting better. I love my costume. I love the way I look in the bearskin coat with a bowler hat tied on with a scarf and boots up to my knees. All I have to do is tramp through the snow with my posse, chasing James Caan. I know how it's going to look on screen. There'll be a shot of Christopher Lambert running through the snow; then one of James Caan with his posse, chasing Christopher; then one of me, with my posse, chasing James. I'll be linked with two stars via the edit. Who cares about the food? And it's a short day. We're using daylight, and it is still winter, so there is not much daylight to use. When we get back, I collect my daily 40 kroner and add it to yesterday's. I go have a beer.

Lunch the next day is a disaster. The caterer hasn't understood the French point of view. His solution to the problem has been to provide more of everything – more bread and cheese, more thin stew. The food at the lodge isn't any better. The French are in a state of disbelief. 'They are poisoning us!' one man hisses to me. The producer runs around trying to smooth things over, promising that a different catering standard will eventually be implemented, if only people will be patient. He is lying.

The French start using hip flasks full of brandy to warm themselves up, and the filming starts to slow down. One-third of the crew is drunk. One-third is freezing and hungry. The Norwegian third is suffering a wounded national pride. The actors, meanwhile, are standing in the snow in thin French shoes worrying about frostbite as the crew drunkenly, hungrily and woundedly fumble over each set-up.

We stand there for hours one day while crew and director argue about a scene in which I get shot by James Caan. They keep setting it up then changing their minds; they want to have it right before they bring Mr Caan out of his trailer. They're happy to keep the rest of us waiting. Besides, they argue, we may as well stand there, we don't have a trailer to go to, one patch of snow is as cold as another.

I'm wondering how this scene will go. We've already had a dialogue rehearsal in which Mr Caan explained that the reason he had no idea where this was in the script was that he didn't read scripts in order to keep fresh for performance. Maybe this works for him, I don't know, but I can foresee another few hours in the snow trying to get the scene right and the dialogue correct, and my feet are already numb to the knees. The only saviour I can think of is the setting of the sun in three hours.

They finally agree on how to do it. Mr Caan is led out of his trailer and shown how the shot will work. He knows his lines now, it's going to happen at last, I am sooo grateful. The stunt involves a gun expert kneeling below the camera and shooting me in the forehead with a blood pellet. They've decided to place the camera about three metres away, and from my peripheral vision the gun looks aimed at my eyes. I find it hard to concentrate. It's me who's fluffing the lines, damn it. We do the shot twice. The first time the gunman hits me in the side of the head. It hurts, but they want to do it again. It has to be the centre of my head, between the eyes, they explain. The gunman doesn't look so sure, he's shaking his head, but they call 'Action!' anyway. The second take, fortunately, is perfect. The gunman laughs out loud, then comes over to explain. He speaks with a cockney accent. 'I've never had to do it from so far away. I was so nervous, the gun kept shaking!' I ask what would have happened if he'd got me in the eye. 'Don't even think about it, mate!' he replies.

Some slow days later, we get to the final scenes in

Rjukan, the horse-riding scenes. Ragnar, our riding instructor, has told us never to gallop in the snow, we are not trained enough to control or react to galloping in the snow, it is too dangerous. This day, he approaches looking worried. Nils the director wants us to ride in, see some corpses, then gallop up the hill and jump over a little ridge on top of it. My co-actors are excited. They are young, athletic, daredevil types. I am terrified. I have visions of broken bones, death, paraplegia, but I say nothing. I don't want to appear a coward. I want the others to like me. 'One last thing,' says Ragnar, 'we've packed the snow tight in a two-metre-wide pathway. Don't let your horse stray off the pathway. The snow is too deep, and the horse could break its legs.'

I focus on gripping the saddle to stay on my horse and get up the hill. I manage the little jump with what I think is remarkable ease. I am full of pride and relief and hope, Ragnar had promised we would do only one take and now that's done. Nils comes over. 'Looked great,' he comments, 'but we need to do it again. Nicholas, you're the sheriff. You're supposed to notice the corpses. That's the point of the scene. When you ride past, could you at least look at them before you gallop off?'

I'm beginning to feel sorry for Nils. The American script doctor has taken to directing some of the scenes. The crew is divided. Everything is going slow, the budget is probably blowing out. And Marty is still fighting for that 'above the line' credit. He's threatening to take me out of the film if we don't get it, and since they've already shot all the Rjukan

173

scenes featuring me, that's a sore point. I'm pretending not to be involved, but Marty's been phoning me to let me know what's happening. I don't know who I sympathise with more, me or Nils. I am beginning to think that an 'above the line' credit isn't such a good idea for this film, that it may have Hollywood backing but Hollywood makes a lot of flops, and maybe it's not worth getting a bad reputation on what looks to be one of them. Besides, I'm having a good time despite the fear and the food and the frozen feet – surely that's what it's really about rather than all this politicking, and anyway I still haven't forgiven Marty for not getting better per diems and paid rehearsals. So I don't complain to Nils about the second take and instead I ring Marty that night and tell him to sign the contract. I don't want to find I've been written out once I get to the Oslo shoot. Then I worry about being a pushover.

When we finish in Rjukan and travel down to the Oslo studios there are already problems with the set. A turn-of-the-19th-century reconstruction of the mining town of Nome, Alaska, has been built, but spring is coming and the snow is melting. Each day the production sends trucks out to collect tons of it from the nearby mountains, bring it back, and spread it on the ground and rooftops. It's supposed to be deep winter. There are hundreds of shivering extras wandering round in 1890s clothes designed by the French. An 18-year-old girl, decked out in a low-cut bodice and suspender-held stockings under a crumpled skirt, stands in the trucked-in snow, her teeth chattering. 'It is my first time in film,' she tells me earnestly, 'and I am a whore!'

The extras have their own catering tent for mealtime. We find out that they are not being fed. They've been asked to bring their own food and told to keep away from the urns that provide tea and coffee. A small rebellion starts to form as actors and crew load up two trays each at lunchtime, and take one each over to the extras' tent. The assistant directors are instructed to stop us doing it, but they don't have the heart. The producers are losing the support of cast and crew. Bad pay, bad food, ruined script and now neglected extras, it's all too much. We share our thin stew and bad coffee as a limp mark of defiance.

By now the shoot is becoming comic. The Parisian actor who plays the general of the army arrives to perform his major scene. He must put the town under military law and order me as sheriff to hunt down James Caan's illegal posse. I am flanked by two assistants, the general by three lieutenants. He speaks with a French accent. 'Shereef,' he says, 'tek some men, and bring back that pussy!' He does not understand why everyone laughs. The script doctor decides to try to help him. 'It's not puusy,' he explains in his American accent, 'it's paarsee.' The Frenchman cannot hear the difference. He attempts it again, copying the Americanised drawl. The result is worse. Nils decides to shoot the scene in close-up because the other actors can't stop laughing. The Frenchman is furious with embarrassment, his performance is excellent. Nils for once is pleased. He tells me that this scene, at least, works. My ears shot up every time the word 'puusy' was mentioned; I looked terrified.

On the day the army and sheriff are supposed to ride into town – a column of 30 or so horse riders entering the street at night in blizzard conditions – one of the assistant directors decides that the horses need to be conditioned to the noise of the wind fans that will generate the blizzard. He sets the fans up in the field beside the horses, turns them on, and leaves for the day. After ten hours, the horses are hysterical and frothing at the mouth with terror and frustration. One of the stunt riders gets thrown and ends up in hospital. It takes most of the night to achieve the shot.

The budget is said to be badly overblown. Mr Caan is rumoured to be behaving in a Hollywood manner, meaning badly. There is unsupported talk of airconditioners ripped out of caravan walls, make-up women reduced to tears. The script has been doctored beyond recognition. Some of the crew are permanently drunk. The production is melting with the snow.

Christopher Lambert works hard to equal the balance. He takes time between shots to talk to members of cast and crew he hasn't yet met, and thank them for their input. He arranges with the other producers for a huge party to raise people's spirits. He turns up on the night but is left standing alone, smiling at the backs of people's heads, a tray of drinks in his hands. No one knows what to say to him, he's a star. He'd been overheard checking on whether Jimmy had used the Lear Jet to go home on the weekend. Jimmy had, it's all over the set. People are wondering if that's why their wages are so low. It's not a life anyone here knows, and anyway most people have given up on the film already and are just accepting the free alcohol while it lasts. But he stays, handing out drinks and complimenting people who do their best to get away as quickly as they can. They can sense it might be a patch-up job.

But none of this affects me. I'm having a ball. Even when Mr Caan delays take after take because he has tight socks; even when the script doctor comes up with bigger and more implausible rewrites each day; even when my feet hurt with the cold because of the silly shoes I have to wear; even when my horse keeps running the opposite way than it's meant to during a take and I'm responsible for hundreds of feet of wasted film; even when I nearly trample a drunk extra who only just manages to escape because a stuntman drags him out of the way of my out-of-control horse; even then I delight in the bizarre theatricality of what I'm doing. The machinery of filmmaking, how it transforms the world and isolates moments, enthrals me. I'm back in that environment where I really have only one responsibility: to perform. And I revel in it.

Paris, winter 1995

It is the beginning of the end already and it's only just started. Paris should be the continuation of the roll, the glorification after the triumph, the icing on the cake, but the clichés have chosen to go in reverse.

Bianca and I are in the Paris office of ABI films, the French distribution company for *Bad Boy Bubby*. Phillipe – 50 or so years old, scraggly grey hair, scrawny body with developing paunch, one of ABI's two directors – is proudly staring at us, as we stare at the box of stickers he has had printed to advertise the film. The stickers make me very, very tired. Phillipe wants to capitalise on my best actor audience awards, accumulated now in Valenciennes and Venice. The stickers will be put on posters and flyers, they have been done just in time for my arrival. He is grinning with the excitement of a job well done.

'NIKE HOPE is BAD BOY BUBBY!' read the stickers, all 1000 of them.

'Phillipe,' I say, 'you've spelt my name like a brand of sneakers.'

'No no,' he laughs. 'It is Nicky, non?'

'No,' I reply, 'it's not. You can't use these.'

'Ha ha! You are so funny,' he says.

I'm weary. This adds to the torpor. I've just been in Paul Cox's film, *Lust and Revenge*, in Adelaide. I can't act. Maybe *Bubby* was it, all my acting potential doused in one fell fluke. I want to blame the director but I'm probably wrong. I've seen the rushes. Unconvincing, flat, wooden, contrived. Maybe the Rjukan experience killed my talent. All those mistakes, all that bad writing, all that involvement in a pointless exercise. Why did I do it? Bloody Norway!

Bianca says it's not Norway. If it's a place, it's Adelaide. She knows because she worked on the film, too, in the costume department. She reckons the shop in the centre of the city with the boarded-up windows and the sign: 'BUSINESS LUNCHES, TOPLESS WAITRESSES, SEE-THROUGH LINGERIE, SHIRT AND TIE A MUST' says it all. A backwater, 30 years out of date, hot, ugly, with violent, redneck, sexist aspirations. She says black comedy is surely the only thing capable of being produced there. I think she's just biased – she had a hard time and her bosses were arseholes. Adelaide's got a lot to offer: you wouldn't get films like *Bubby* made elsewhere! She says, 'Exactly, nowhere else would generate the idea.'

Whatever it is, it's punctured my confidence. Paris should be a retreat. A paid publicity junket for both of us. A place to replenish the creative streak with sycophantic press in the middle of artistic, romantic Paris. I feel I need it. I want Bianca to see it. My regrowth has to be observed to be useful. Nike Hope is a bad start.

Sabine, who is Phillipe's wife and ABI's other director, enters the room. Short, rotund, big hair, big jewellery. Mr and Mrs Jack Spratt. Sabine acts as the welcoming committee. We must be tired, she says, it's so good we could come, we must go to the hotel, we must eat, we must meet Jean, the investor who is funding the film's release, sit down, she will just make a few phone calls. Take a seat, take a seat, it won't be long.

We sit, jet-lagged, with our luggage. They make phone calls. Paris waits outside. The office is crammed, hot, stuffy. Sabine waves occasionally and Phillipe laughs good-naturedly. I try to say something, get the name of the hotel, anything, but they wave me down. Not long, not long, they repeat.

Depression looms. We huddle like refugees in the corner, waiting for attention. Another hour passes then Sabine hangs up the phone, shouts in French at Phillipe, motions us to follow and heads down the stairs. She ushers us into the back of a small car crammed into a smaller space in a street too narrow to manoeuvre. She loads our cases on top of us, squeezes into the front passenger seat. We wait 20 minutes for Phillipe, who hasn't followed, while Sabine tells us that we are fighting for cinemas, the major distributors have a stranglehold, but we have a few key locations for the release. They are dependent on how much publicity I can generate, we will be busy.

'Can we have a schedule?' I ask.

'No no,' Sabine laughs, 'we will call you.'

Phillipe slides himself into the car and they shout at each other as he bumps his way out of the parking spot and drives 500 metres to our hotel on the Champs Élysées. 'We could have walked,' I say. They laugh.

Phillipe points to the room tariff on the door.

'Expensive,' he says. Then: 'We will eat. Just wait. We will phone you. Don't go out.'

It is the order of the next two days. Incarceration in a small, slightly comfortable, expensive room without food on the Champs Élysées. They don't phone. Either the publicity isn't happening or it has fallen through, but no, they say, just stay there, we will call. Occasionally they come to feed us, nodding when we ask for vegetarian and taking us to a selection of steakhouses. We view Paris from the hotel window. This is it, I think, this is my life: always on the edge looking in. One accidentally good performance in a film that promises the world and delivers a hotel room.

On the second night Bianca has had enough – of me or the room, who knows – and confronts Sabine and Phillipe in French. There is an argument, gesticulation, shouting around the steakhouse table. The next day, there is a schedule and per diems. Finally, the publicity starts.

This is what I came for. I can sense my soul being refilled. The press love the film. They love me. They take photos, praise me, ask about my family life, about my preparation as an actor, about Rolf. Radio interviewers ask me to repeat lines from the film. A hopeful director takes me out to a derelict site and films me going around corners in slow motion for a TV segment on Canal Plus. I am introduced as the new Brando at a question-and-answer session for a university screen studies course. I introduce the film at cinemas around Paris, and sign autographs. I am an actor, a good actor, I have a future, everyone tells me so. It's a familiar place to be and it's comfortable and it's reassuring, and it's the French who are saying it in the shadow of the Eiffel Tower and Notre Dame and The Louvre. It must be true. 'Was I really as bad as I think in *Lust and Revenge*?'

I ask Bianca. 'Or was I just affected by the fact that we were having a bad time?'

'We were having a bad time. You can't judge your performance until you see the whole film,' she answers. How right. How silly of me to think I was so bad when I haven't seen the performance in context. Remember *Bubby* and how I thought I was bad in that? I was wrong then, I'm probably wrong now. Everyone is their own worst critic – it's part of the artistic temperament.

I knew this was a good move. Bianca is looking after the French side of things: if I have complaints or trouble understanding, she translates or fixes. It's good practice, she hasn't spoken French in a while. I appreciate it and I'm sure she does too – it allows her to improve her French, and me to concentrate on the interviews. *Would I like to work in Europe?* Absolutely, I recently finished a film with James Caan in Norway. I consider Europe a second home. I'd particularly like to work in France, in fact I've just signed with an agent in the UK to facilitate working in that trans-hemisphere way – Peters Fraser and Dunlop, you may have heard of them, they're very big. *Do you enjoy working in Europe?* Oh yes, I'm very lucky to be able to do so. I have a European passport, and the different acting and directing styles are so educative, it stretches and expands my capabilities as an artist. *And if you worked in France, which French directors would you most like to work with?* There are so many it's difficult to isolate just a few . . .

We meet Jean, the investor. He's a property developer with an interest in film. He has a silver Rolls Royce and a chauffeur and a five-storey house in the centre of Paris with a swimming pool at the bottom and a private cinema on top. He looks like the character of Bubby gone rich: bald on top with thin, screwball hair on the sides, a huge chin, soft voice, loose, baggy black clothes. He wants to buy *Bubby* for the American market but reshoot the outdoor scenes in New York or Paris to make it look like a city instead of a graveyard. The film's producers, he says, don't understand. I'm with him all the way. He wants to finance whatever my next film is, I'll do whatever it takes. I give him a script called *Killer Jones* that's been sent to me and he hires a translator. He's interested, he rings the Australian producers. My God, I may have just got my next lead role financed.

I'm infatuated. Jean gives me an African statuette that stands by the side of the pool as a gift. Jean is in consultation with French playwrights and actors and directors about all their next shows. Jean has a major office block/hotel/shopping complex in development further along the Champs Élysées. Jean has different pretty young women escorts every night we join him for dinner. Cooking. Speaking English. Playing the hostess when we leave. Waving goodbye to us from the door. Never to be seen again, replaced by someone new the next day. Even Bianca is fascinated.

I'm more inclined to be lenient in my judgement of Phillipe and Sabine. The publicity has been good, the film has opened well, and they have impressive friends. Perhaps I'm just being very Anglo about Gallic ways of doing things.

When they ask me to spend the last day travelling with them to an outlying town that is exhibiting *Bubby* and would love a visit from its star, I agree. What better way to end the tour? Bianca, in a prescient move, chooses to change her ticket and visit friends in London instead. That's okay, I tell her, I'll be fine.

We are scheduled to catch a train to the town at two p.m. Phillipe changes his mind at 1.55. We will drive, it will be quicker, just wait in the office. I do. I wait until five. The film, I know, is starting at seven and I am supposed to introduce it. No problem, says Phillipe, the car is fast! We leave at six. Paris is gridlocked with peak-hour traffic. We get on to one of the ring roads by seven. Sabine rings the cinema, who put the film off until eight. By then we are halfway there but Sabine is screaming at Phillipe in English – for my benefit – telling him he is going the wrong way. The cinema rings to ask where we are, and agrees to show the film and have a question-and-answer session afterwards. At nine we pass the sign indicating the turn-off for the township, but Phillipe is shouting at Sabine that it is the wrong turn-off, he knows there is a better one, we will drive until we find it. Their screaming lapses into French. By ten or so we have turned back from the German border and Sabine is answering the call from the cinema and taking directions from them. She stays on the mobile for the hour it takes to get back to the turn-off, and for the extra half hour it takes to get to the cinema.

The manager runs out waving a torch in illuminated semaphore. The film is over and they have kept the audience waiting an hour and a half with regular reports as to where we are. So far no one has left, they are eager to meet the star of *Bad Boy Bubby*, but first I must put my handprint in the wet concrete square they have laid in the cinema plaza in remembrance of tonight. I get photographed on my hands and knees, with a poster behind me and one of Phillipe's stickers plastered over it. Somewhere in suburban France, Nike Hope's handprint decorates a cinema floor.

At last we enter the cinema. The crowd cheers and claps. It is the most massive cinema screen I have come across. These people would have had an excruciating time. I am tired and angry and my body feels atrophied, but I attempt to be charming as I introduce myself and Phillipe and Sabine, then ask if anyone has any questions. After this uncharted squabble across the freeways of France with these two, I am hopeful of some sort of intelligent appraisal of my talents, and of the poignant piece of art I see myself as promoting. A young woman puts up her hand, and in a halting French accent asks, 'Do you as an actor really like big breasts?' And then she giggles.

Sochi, summer 1996

Bianca is laughing, holding a bunch of flowers while standing outside the Hotel Zhemchuzhina. The Russian boy who gave them to her kneels on one leg, and balances his guitar on the other. He is singing Russian love songs full of saccharine Aryan references to beautiful Nordic eyes. I refuse to believe Bianca is being taken in, but who knows, she's certainly allowing it to happen. This boy's leeched on to her from day one. I can feel I'm being watched watching in red humiliation. My sleeve is tugged. Russian Crooner has tried to distract me by sending his friend's teenage wife who wants to dance in the emptied swimming pool, but I'm not falling for that. This slimeball just won't stop. I know his game even if Bianca refuses to admit it. He's been following us around for days. He's looking for a brush with celebrity, a fantasy fling, free party entrance, maybe a ticket out of here. How dare he!

I'm not going to be undignified about this. Bianca is flattered, that's all. The boy is pretty in a certain way, though short and coiffeured with a wavery voice and far too creamily macho a presentation for my liking, but hey, that's just taste. I'm not going to be undignified because I am an important guest here, a jury member for the Sochi International Film Festival on the Black Sea in Russia. I am standing with members of the jury now; they are watching me to see my reaction, or at least I think they are. I am so prized a guest the festival has paid for Bianca to come as well. They have flown both of us over from Norway. Bianca is taking a break from writing and work to be my official consort if you will. The least she can do is act the part. Her public behaviour reflects on me.

But my reaction to it reflects more. After this I've got two films coming up, in New York and Spain. I'm truly on my way now. Mere twinges of jealousy shouldn't intrude. I have to be international, a man of the world. The French contingent has already been sent home, several with black eyes, after getting into a tussle with the Mafioso-looking Russian festival security over the payment of restaurant bills. I don't want to be sent home. I turn back to my group of jurors and smile. Russian Crooner isn't worth it. He is just a dull ebb in the otherwise bizarre, elite glitter of the Sochi Film Festival, and I am an invited guest.

The town is a resort located on the Black Sea, a ferry's ride from Istanbul, with sulphur baths, hotels, subtropical climate, subtropical beaches. In its heyday it was used as a way to reward approved workers with a free resort-style holiday. It catered to over five million sponsored visitors annually. Since perestroika, numbers have reduced to half a million. There are mouldering husks of concrete buildings hugging the shoreline. 'People began building them just before the collapse,' explained the guidebook. 'Then the money ran out. You can buy a building very cheap!' The Sochi Film Festival is an attempt to revitalise the town, and to bring attention to the Russian films that screen beside the international films. This year it is heavily funded by Boris Yeltsin, who is facing an election in which the rival Communist Party looks like winning. Boris is spending big.

The only Russian people who can afford the town or the

festival now are those with money. Prostitutes travel here to tan in preparation for the Moscow summer season, accompanied by their grey-suited pimps. Russian Mafia types saunter by with bodyguards. Russian business people, Russian stars, Russian celebrities of all kinds arrive to see and be seen. The Russian press hangs around the hotel lobby and the beach. It is a prestige Russian event. Sochi locals haven't a hope in hell of getting in by themselves, though they try to by attaching themselves to foreign dignitaries. The Crooner is just one of many. He did it at the opening ceremony, now he's trying again at the closing. Singing his heart out for a ticket.

We are near the main entrance of the concrete towerblock hotel, which overlooks the beach on one side and the Olympic-size swimming pool on the other. Crowds are gathering for the closing ceremony. The emptied pool is being closed off for party preparations. Crooner's friend's teenage wife looks disappointed and is pouting. Swarthy men with machine guns guard the hotel doors. There is an advert for the upstairs snooker room displayed in the window, a young woman leaning over the pool table, her cleavage exposed by her low-cut singlet, her posterior and vulva exposed in the full-length mirror behind her, clutching a snooker cue suggestively and smiling at the camera. Beside her, the festival poster bears the slogan: 'Welcome to the Sochi International Film Festival 1996!' Below that are the names, in Russian, of all the invited guests. *Invited* is the key word. Brando, Pacino, Hanks, De Niro, Pitt, Sarandon, Davies, the list goes on. My name, I am told, is on there somewhere.

The jury is assembled on the footpath. Swedish director Bo Widerberg is the jury president. I am the only Australian. The rest are a collection of people from all over east and west Europe. One of them, a woman from Berlin, has her arm in a sling. She broke it coming off her Aeroflot flight. I'm pleased Bianca and I refused to fly Aeroflot. We jurors have spent the day in Stalin's *dacha*, arguing over the distribution of festival prizes after posing together for a photo with a wax sculpture of the man himself. Eastern Europe is big on wax sculptures. There have been a series of compromises. I have had to give up my choice of best actor in order to win my choice of best actress. Because she got best actress, the film she is in won't get second prize. Because of the film chosen as winner, another film has been included in the prize-getters to mollify the Ukrainian judges who disagreed vehemently with the main decision. We gather in a disgruntled group now, trying to be polite. I attempt not to be distracted by Bianca and the Crooner. The president of the jury tries to amuse us by telling of the local screening he just attended of his own film. 'They turn the sound down,' he explains, 'and have a woman at the front screaming all the lines out in Russian.'

'We know,' say the Ukrainians.

The pathway from the hotel to the main theatre has been cleared of its usual occupants to help glamorise the event. Normally it is lined by people selling various items. For a few roubles, or preferably a single American dollar, it is possible to buy a plastic supermarket bag, a single shoe, the cover of a book, a glove, various soft-drink bottles filled with clear, homemade alcohol. We have found it too distressing to face, we go the back way, via the private beach where the sellers can't get past the guards. But today we don't need to worry. This is a crème-de-la-crème gathering.

There is a lot of flesh on display. It would be easy to mistake it for a pornography festival; the woman in the poster looks modest in comparison. See-through body stockings, fish-net dresses, leather and studs, thick layers of blue and pink make-up. I've started to get used to it; it's become attractive. Bianca nearly bought one of the dresses, and her make-up today is thicker than normal. It must be catching, or else she's pandering to the Russian boy.

I'm still watching her. She's dressed in a striking red suit – in lieu of the dress she didn't buy – and is being asked for autographs. I don't think she should give them, it's all false pretences, she's not who they think she is. Crooner hangs around in the background. She doesn't seem to be paying him much attention but he's still there, guitar at the ready. Bianca is asking people what they would like written on their autographs. One girl replies, 'Uma Thurman!'

An American we met on the beach is here for the ceremony. He's spied Crooner and is talking to him and Bianca. I wish he'd stop. I wave but don't know why. He has a hand in my growing aggravation. He introduced himself as a resident of the area a couple of days into the festival. He explained he liked to entertain the foreign celebrities each year. He said he recognised us from the publicity material –

wasn't I an actor? He'd seen my film last year. He was having a party that night, a number of people were attending, would we like to come?

I was flattered. He seemed a little odd, but he was going out of his way, how could I refuse? He would pick us up at six and drive us to his house, a little place he and his wife had bought 'for a steal' on the outskirts of Sochi, and were now 'doing up'.

The house was grey and foreboding and hollow. The 'doing up' hadn't really started. It stood on its own in a paddock, two donkeys by the wall, one standing, the other collapsed on its side, kicking feebly and wheezing. The American wasn't sure what was wrong with it. He thought maybe it was dying, it'd been like that for days. Around the back was the barbecue, a hole in the ground filled with wood and leaves that was used later to cook bloody meat from a bucket. Inside, his young Russian wife stood waiting to greet us beneath a full-length supermarket-style nude painting of herself. She and the American tried to interest Bianca in having one done, the artist was a friend of theirs and it would only take an hour.

We were the only non-USSR guests present, and we were a popular celebrity attraction. Everyone wanted to talk to us. We got statistics: the majority of surveyed high-school girls in Moscow in 1995 said that their preferred job would be foreign-currency prostitute; the majority of boys responded that theirs would be to join the Russian Mafia. We got jokes: after the next election, Yeltsin is told there is bad news and good news – the bad news is that the

Communists got 55 per cent of the vote. The good news is that Yeltsin got 60 per cent.

And then we got Russian Crooner.

I was pissed off as soon as he arrived. I already recognised him. He'd singled us out before, at the opening-night party. We'd spent that day watching, from our window, the Olympic-size swimming pool being emptied, and trestle tables being placed around it in rows. We'd been told to get to the gates by eight p.m. to be allowed in as jury, but by that time the whole of Sochi was already lined up, and Crooner and friends made their first appearance. He attached himself to Bianca, begged her to say he was her official translator. No problem. All the festival guests had local translators, it's how the locals got in. I understood, it only seemed fair. I had two very pretty ones myself.

The gates finally opened at eleven p.m. The crowd surged in, dived at the tables, and started to strip them of the contents – bottles of vodka lined three deep. We could see them disappearing. We grabbed a few too, and hid some more under the special screened-off jury table. Our local 'translators' had disappeared, we thought that was the last we would see of them. Speeches started on the stage at the head of the empty pool but no one was watching or listening because fireworks were set off at the same time at the other end, so close people were squealing for cover. The whole crowd was on a vodka high by the time the band arrived, mobbed by screaming teenagers. 'Watch them,' shouted one jury member, 'they are the hottest Russian pop act around. They are why *Priscilla, Queen of the Desert* isn't funny!'

The boy band somersaulted on to the stage, all ten of them, in garish feather costumes – feathered heads, shoulders, nipples, groins. They sang while performing acrobatic tricks, they had sex with their feathers, they looked like a multi-million-dollar drag act, and the girls in the audience were fighting to get at them. 'See?' shouted the jury member. 'It's normal for our singers to dress like that. For the Russians, there was no joke!' Some other act started before the band was finished, a DJ, but it didn't matter, people were too drunk to notice. We ended up in a Swiss banker's bedroom and somehow Crooner had followed us and there he was, drinking the banker's Swiss cognac and talking to Bianca, while the director of a Swiss film in competition tried to bribe me with dinner invitations to vote for his film.

And there Crooner was again, at the American's house, being more insistent over the barbecue of bloody bucket meat. He'd brought his guitar. He serenaded my girlfriend. He sang love songs to her. The Russians all clapped and whooped. 'Hasn't he got a lovely voice?' they said. 'And look, your girlfriend, she is blushing, she loves it. He is young, you are old, you'd better watch out or she will fall for his moody Russian passion! You are English, you have no hair, if I were you I'd be worried!'

Worried? Unlikely. I'd seen Bianca's eyes when the American stood up, spread his arms to encompass the barren pasture, the dying donkey, the grey, ominous block-of-concrete house, and in a quavering voice stated, 'How could I go back to the US after this? Look at it! My own little piece of paradise!' I could see the embarrassment on

193

her face once the Crooner started singing. I felt safe in the certainty of a ticket out of here. The security of knowing that she knew I would never subject her to the indignity of being serenaded by cheesy love songs in public, never make her the uncomfortable subject of everyone's expectation. Amorous threat was not the worry. It was the territorial infringement that was causing my discomfiture.

Then and now. Here in front of the Hotel Zhem-chuzhina, on the last day of the festival. He was and is being indiscreet. Bianca is accepting his indiscretion. That's why he feels safe to give her flowers and to sing to her in front of the public and the jury. She should reject him. Acceptance is more false pretence. It's not good for my image. I have a developing status to maintain. This is *my* gig.

Outside the hotel the crowd starts to move towards the theatre and Bianca joins me. 'Did you like that?' I ask sharply. 'Did you like being sung at in public by that smarmy idiot who's been following you round like a lap dog for the past two weeks?'

'Don't be silly, it's just sweet. It's the function we have here,' she laughs. 'You've no idea how many different celebrities' names I just signed!'

Armed guards halt us a long way away from the theatre. Russian glitterati are arriving. They're the equivalent, one jury member tells me, of the Beatles and the Rolling Stones and the Royal Family. The crowd of spectators and guests stretches into the distance, but the guards are making sure only one small group goes up the red carpet at a time so that the TV cameras can get maximum coverage. This is going to take hours. I should have known. The organisation here has been catastrophic.

When at last we are ushered into the festival theatre, I see the Swiss director from the opening night trying to catch my eye. I'm glad I didn't go to dinner with him because the film was awful. I'd gone to the circus with Bianca instead, and we'd watched a car and a bikini-clad woman get raffled off in the middle of the animal acts. The raffle had been fixed by a Mafia man who wanted everyone to see his new car; it was so much more exciting than dinner with the boring Swiss filmmaker. I turn around to avoid catching his eye, and blow me down I can see Crooner making his way up the red carpet. How did he get in here?

It's a massive edifice, this theatre, and the foyer is packed like a gas oven. I recognise some of the flesh being crushed against me. These people have been sunbathing each day on the private beach, standing in the sun as they do, arms akimbo like penguins, turning around every half hour to even the exposure. I can see Crooner trying to make his way over to us, but I am Jury so we get ushered through ahead of the hoi polloi. Ha! The walls are lined with guards and cameramen. It takes a long time to get everyone seated. Then the huge billowing red curtains sweep back, and a giant model pearl rolls on to the stage and jerkily opens to orchestral music. There is a dancer inside dressed as a fairy. The crowd cheers and stomps. I start to get interested when it looks like she might be about to perform some kind of striptease, but then we jury members are summoned by a guard to follow him backstage and wait for our cue. We are unsure what will happen when it comes.

We stand there for most of the presentation, and the woman with the broken arm nearly faints, but when we try to take her to a chair the guard gestures us back with his machine gun. Finally we are led on to the stage, presented, and led off again, and we make our way through the foyer back to our seats, a difficult business of convincing the layers of guards at each door that we are the jury, the international jury, we are invited guests, yes of course, check with the director. I sit down and look at Bianca in her red suit, then at the audience in various stages of Mafia grey and pornographic undress, then at the procession of prize winners from Turkey, Iran, France, the Ukraine. I forget for a moment about Crooner and am taken back to speech day at St Luke's when the school prizes got given out. The feeling wasn't so different from this, though the clothing was far more conservative. Everyone wanted their son to win a prize. It was very important, if you were a part of the small college community.

Crooner finds us at the party afterwards. How did he get in? 'I am so sorry,' he tells me, and asks Bianca to dance. 'I am so sorry,' he says again, and sits down with us. 'I am so sorry,' he says, and tries to follow us back to the hotel and into our room. What does he want, a threesome? I fight with Bianca about him in between saying goodbye to jury members who I am trying to give my details to so they will employ me. I want her to know this is my reputation we're dealing with here, but she can't see that, she says she's just being friendly, I have no right. It escalates. 'There's friendly and there's friendly,' I shout.

'What did you want me to do?' she yells.

'You should know!' I riposte.

'Hit him?' she bellows, but by then there's only an hour before the flight to Moscow and we haven't packed, so we have to stop fighting to coordinate our departure. I'm hung-over and I haven't even slept.

'Aeroflot. No choice,' says the guide, 'it's that or nothing.' Small pieces of metal hang off the plane. We shuffle on in horror. The seats are all rotting. I hear someone moaning loudly, 'We're all going to die! We're all going to die!' It's me.

We get to our seats but someone is in them. The single flight attendant shrugs her shoulders. 'So sit somewhere else!' she says. I sit down and put on my seat belt, but the headache – I need a pill, I need my bag. I stand up and the seat comes with me. I start moaning again. The last passenger comes on with his three personal security guards, all carrying submachine guns. 'Fucking hell,' someone whispers behind me.

The only life jacket is the one being used in the demonstration. There is a sign by Bianca's head advising passengers to pull the rope hanging from the wall in case of an emergency. 'There is no rope, Bianca,' I say, 'there is no rope! THERE IS NO ROPE!' Our argument is forgotten, Crooner is forgotten. The plane takes off vertically and I think I scream but it could just be in my head, and when it levels out the flight attendant gives out quarter cups of warm Pepsi before vanishing. I am in pain. The plane rattles, everyone is pale. This, I think, could be it. I'm about to die. I need to tell someone, but Bianca is asleep. I can't bear to wake her, it would be too, too cruel, but then maybe I should, it could be my last chance. We go into a suicide dive without warning, and I can see the ground approaching fast, and Bianca wakes and there is someone screaming, but it isn't either of us, we're too petrified, then the next thing we know we've levelled out and landed and everyone is clapping like they do in America, but here I understand.

The full moon shines over Red Square. A group of youths stands and howls skywards. The clock chimes midnight. The Aladdin-style domes pulse with vibrant colour. It's another world. A different kind of extremity. In the hotel, prostitutes wait next to, and in, the elevators. An American dog-collared cleric has a group of them around his table. He is feeding them, and lecturing them in slow, simple English. 'So when I am naughty,' he says, 'God spanks me!' They nod and eat. He's paying.

Moscow Airport the next day is full of soldiers. One of them is in the toilets trying to hide the fact that he has no socks, that his feet are bloody, that he is wrapping toilet paper around them. The paper goes red as he tries to put his boots back on. I pretend not to look – he doesn't want me to see, it's a loss of status, and I have a ticket out of here and there's nothing to be gained by exploiting my luck.

Outside, Bianca is saying goodbye to the chauffeur. 'We were so excited to be here,' she gushes.

'We were so excited to have you,' he replies in monotone as he walks off. Inside, the airport staff ignore us.

'When will the plane leave?' we ask.

'You will know!' they answer, and wave us away. The shop assistant refuses to sell us a drink because he is closing up.

Panic. It is the familiar world of non-celebrity. We have devalued as we travelled. But it doesn't matter. I am alive, I am escaping. And I have work coming.

New York, spring 1997

The man with the facial tic is pointing aggressively at Bianca while his lips pucker and blow random kisses in every direction. I think he's flirting at first, but if so he's being indiscriminate. He shakes his finger accusingly. 'You think you're pretty, but you got nothin' on my girlfriend. She's a model. A Russian model. You got nothin' on her!' He blows a kiss, glazes over, sparks up again. 'Russian. That's why I've been in Azerbaijan.'

He's a millionaire, he says so, and he's buying us drinks because we are the handsomest couple in the Dublin House this fine evening. He's been coming here for years, it's the best bar in New York, they gave him credit when he was low. Credit when he was low! They didn't desert him and he won't desert them. Now, we might be handsome but he can tell we're not rich, and he is! Azerbaijan, you know what he did there? He bought all the chicken farms, that's what he did, because he's a good businessman, a smart investor, and they've got oil. It's only a matter of time before those fields are developed and they'll be bigger than Saudi Arabia and when they are what do you think those Azerbaijanis are gonna wanna eat? They're gonna wanna eat chicken, that's what, and they're gonna have to buy it off him, and by God if he's rich now he'll be loaded then.

The bar is filling up and it seems safe to turn away, his attention is drifting. New York is full of these people, soaring ambitions high on their own importance and success. It surges up through the pavement into your toes, an adrenaline rush that makes it hard to sleep, though maybe that's just the traffic noise. Somehow it's cushioning me through the slap down I've just had from the writer/potential director of the script *Killer Jones*, who has phoned to say that he can't get an Australian distributor to commit to the film unless he drops me from the lead role. They want someone younger, or more famous, and no it doesn't matter that the role is written for me and for my age. Youth or a name and preferably both, so although I have by now got both Jean in France and Showtime in Australia interested in investing, I'm dropped. He's really sorry but that's how it is and he's sure we'll work together sometime in the future.

That's okay. It's a loss, but I'm working. In New York! City of energy and ambition, and with a personal idol, Hal Hartley. Surely that beats a thriller in Perth with an unknown. It may not be a lead role but it is a realised ambition and it came about through initiative. This city is so affirming. A letter, written and proofread by Bianca, sent via Marty, with a video, suggesting we work together. And voilà! Here I am. Seven days spread over six weeks at $466 a day with no airfare or accommodation supplied and I pay for the relevant visas, so even though I've got a grant from the Australian Film Commission to help out it ends up costing me US$1000 to do the film, but who cares? *Hal Hartley* will be on my CV, it's a career move.

We leave the Dublin House on 79th and pass the man who always walks his pet monitor lizard after midnight, and make our way to the Snug Bar on Amsterdam, where another man buys us a drink and tells us he's a biochemist working on a cure for HIV. He's very close. Previous research concentrated on ways to trick the body into thinking it had no protease, which was what the virus attached to, whereas his research looked into linking a hydrogen molecule to the protease, making the protease unrecognisable to the virus, so it linked to the hydrogen and became inactive. But he couldn't get support. His research would provide a cure and put the drug companies out of business, the US government and US drug companies were trying to block him, so he was working with the French. You win some, you lose some, he says.

It's getting late and this is Bianca's last day in New York, so we go back to our studio apartment on the Upper East side. The janitor, as usual, pretends not to see us. She knows I'm illegally subletting the apartment from a friend of a friend in the production office, at twice the rent she pays. It's supposed to be furnished, with cable TV, but the friend has moved everything out and I've had to beg sheets, blankets and furniture from the office staff. Since I'm not on the janitor's list of tenants she doesn't want to know.

I had tried, on first arriving, to arrange for messages to be kept for me, but she refused. 'But I'll be here for the next six weeks,' I protested. 'Listen,' she answered, 'I don't know you're here, so you're not here.'

There was a pull-down 'Murphy' bed in the room, and a cord in the corner, which was presumably for the cable TV I was paying for. I didn't know how this worked but every now and again real estate people let themselves in while I was still asleep and showed people around. I was amazed at how few people were put off by the naked man in the bed. The room was so small the bed took most of the space, it wasn't as if they could miss seeing me. They didn't even acknowledge my being there, the agents just flicked a card on the bed as they left. It was a popular room: it overlooked the Dakota building where Madonna had an apartment, where *Rosemary's Baby* was filmed, and where John Lennon was assassinated. Central Park was just down the street one way, a metro station the other. A lot of people wanted to rent it. I passed each of the cards on to the office.

It was dispiriting living in a cleared-out apartment without work for six days a week. Alone except for sudden unannounced visits from unseeing wannabe tenants. Dumped from a script written for me because I was too old and too unknown. Overwhelmed by the unceasing clamour of the city. Worried about finances and whether the Spanish film would confirm. Worried that maybe I shouldn't be doing a small role. And then Bianca arrived, for two weeks.

She had a list of things to do and see. She had news of the film in Spain – it was definitely going ahead, I should hear soon, and besides she'd be working on it. She was full of support for doing a small role in a Hal Hartley film, she thought it a wonderful career move. She was excited by the city. She thought it fantastic I only worked one day a week. She thought the apartment was great and the Murphy bed a stunner. She knew where the Dublin House was, and the Snug Bar, and the White Horse Inn where Dylan Thomas drank himself to death. She knew which art galleries to visit and which markets and which bookshops. She'd done the research. She knew and found the New York we wanted to see. How come I couldn't? I could imagine living here now. I love the New York Bianca found.

'A strapping specimen of a woman' was how the lead actor described her over lunch on one of my working days. It was his first feature film, and we had a lot in common. He was buoyed and insecure all at once. I didn't know whether I felt more sympathy for or jealousy towards him. He wasn't getting the attention he deserved. From my point of view he was giving all he'd got to the film. When Hartley called 'Cut!' he was still acting, he carried the action through to its natural conclusion, but he was opposite someone who appeared to freeze in motion and who didn't seem to be listening to the other actors. It made everything very difficult. And this other guy was getting all the attention and all the accolades when rushes were shown. I was sympathetic. There must have been some paranoic stress building up, there would have been if I were in his position. At the same time he was the lead and I was this tiny support role, so it was hard to feel too much sympathy, I'd have killed to be in his position. Every now and again I wondered if he was wondering why I was doing such a small role, why I'd travelled all the way over here and paid so much money to work one day a week in a New York independent film, if he thought I was stupid. I liked it that he chose to sit beside me at lunch. I liked it that my girlfriend rated with him. I liked the status it conveyed between him and I as men and actors, the covert recognition of my prestige. I accepted the compliment graciously. 'Yeah, she's great,' I replied.

Even after Bianca leaves, New York maintains its excitement. I know what to eat, what to drink, where to go. I don't understand how it could ever have been so intimidating. Hey, I feel like a local now.

Meanwhile the film is sailing along. The crew have all worked on Hartley's films before, they are used to the style, quick at creating set-ups. The camera rarely moves, all the action happens through choreography and timing, so most of the work is in the rehearsals. The actors seem to have watched all of Hartley's films and are aping the Hartley 'style'. He spends a lot of time trying to get past it, it's becoming too studied. He refers everyone to the diaries of French philosopher/playwright Antonin Artaud, to a section where Artaud has been released from therapy but wants back in, because the 'sanity' the therapy has given him is rooted in a lack of emotions or beliefs, and Artaud wants his emotions and beliefs back. That, says Hartley, is the film. The community has no beliefs, no morality, no sanity, and the character of Henry Fool is the catalyst that forces them to create one, even if it is at the expense of being seen as insane. The actors need to find that emotional truth. He will find the style.

That's all very well, but my first six days are mute and it's only on the last that we do all my speaking sections. All thought of truth or style is out the window as I realise this is it: my chance to shine in a Hal Hartley film in front of all these other New York actors who know I've bust my gut to get here and do this and now here I am, on the line. It had been so difficult getting here. The 01 Working Visa was a nightmare. I had a conviction from years ago, for stealing condoms. The lawyer who charged US$400 an hour to get the visa said I should declare it – if I didn't and they found out, then I was dead meat. The 01 was approved but the entry visa wasn't. I was guilty of a crime of moral turpitude in the US government's eyes, I had to apply for a 'waiver of ineligibility'. 'What do they want?' I asked the lawyer. 'Do I need to write a letter promising not to steal any more condoms?' The approval came through the day before I left. I'd packed and paid in blind faith, but then on arrival in the country two fat men in uniforms with moustaches and guns sat me in customs next to a chair with handcuffs attached as a grisly hint, and grilled me for an hour about my history of crime. This is the States, they said, we don't like dishonesty here. It was hard not to laugh, but fear helped. All that and now here's the moment.

I don't have that many words to say but those I do I keep muddling up. People laugh at first, but it stops being funny very quickly. Parker Posey, the female lead, tries to lighten things up by saying, 'Who cares what he says, he's got such a cute accent!' I stop, take a breath, think it through, see my idol looking at me stonily. Think of the post office, St Luke's, the desert, childbirth, the lifespan of the sun, the expansion and contraction of the universe, the difficulty of getting to this point. Today is a pretty small event, it's not worth this nausea, it doesn't even hurt, for God's sake. As Bianca said, it can only do good.

When it's all finished I walk back to the apartment. The beggar who's been outside the hotel on my street for the whole six weeks tells me why he's there. The manager of the hotel once gave him a job as a doorman, but the locals complained. They recognised him as the beggar who used to be on the street, and they told the manager that having a beggar as a doorman brought both the hotel and the neighbourhood down. The manager agreed to take the job away. So the beggar decided he was going to stand there day and night, and keep on bringing them down. You've got to keep your optimism, he tells me.

In the morning I stagger past the janitor with my suitcases. She calls out, 'Are you leaving?' I tell her yes. She comes out from behind her desk, apologises for not talking, I must know what it's like, rules are rules, next time I'm in town I must drop in, she's been here for years and God knows she'll be here for years more! She'll get the taxi for me, if she does I'll get a better rate. So where do I come from? Australia! My God, she'd love to go there, and am I going back? No! To Spain! Lordy! You know what, her family comes from there, well you know not really but generations back . . .

Getting out is easy. Quick stamps in the passport, hardly a second look. It's all so different from getting in. Was it worth the effort? It doesn't matter any more, it's done, and now *Hartley* truly is on my CV. And I think I did okay in the end, and Spain is confirmed and well paid – I'm on my way there now, and Bianca has gone ahead, and this is a support lead role, written for me. Of course the Hartley was worth it, it shows I'm a serious actor, it gives me more international credits, it shows I select my work according to the full work not just the size of the role. Isn't that the way it should be? Isn't that the truth?

nicholas hope

Vigo, summer 1997

The New York biochemist was right: you win some, you lose some. Just before the Hartley film, there'd been a meeting in LA with the board of New Line, who told me that they'd been split 50/50 between me and Kevin Spacey for the role of the killer in *Seven*. I've been reading about the film. I've just realised what a loss that was. Life would have been a different reality had I got the part, and surely Spacey didn't need the role? But now here I am being congratulated on my professionalism on a film in Spain. I've just done my first scene walking down a street, and the director of photography and the director's assistant and the director himself have all come over and told me, 'Nicholas, you claimed the character with that walk.' It's a good feeling, I've worked hard to create this character's physicality, and I've had a say in the costume, which is nearly overstated but not quite. Bushy sideburns, a silver tooth, wispy long hair, tight red jeans, tight fawn leather jacket. I agree: I know this character, I've helped create him, I'm really working. I've found my niche.

We're setting up now for a fight scene, but there's no fight coordinator or safety person on set, so Bent, the director, has asked me to choreograph it. It's pretty simple, it's all out of focus in the background, but I'm still chuffed with the responsibility. Bent is off discussing the shot and I've gathered the three people who are going to beat me up to show them what I want. It's past two a.m, we're in the town square, we're trying to be as quiet as we can, but people are still leaning out of windows shouting at us to shut up, they need to sleep. Anita the second assistant director is shouting back: shut up yourselves, if you leave us be we'll be out of here sooner you deadshits. I've been studying Spanish – I can understand some of what she says because she's speaking Catalan, though most of the people here speak Galician. I hadn't thought of that.

Two of the people beating me up are actors, but the third one is a painter Bent liked the look of. He's nervous and he's been drinking. He's brought some of his paintings to the set in an attempt to impress the female members of the crew, but they haven't responded. Now he thinks he can impress by being a method actor. He doesn't want to learn how to pull his punches, it's not real, he says, he doesn't pull punches, he just hits hard, heh heh. It's a worry, so I make him practise with the other two who tell him they'll kill him if he touches them. I decide not to rehearse with him, just to do the first take, but when we do he belts me in the solar plexus and I double over. The other two think I'm acting and haul me upright and he goes to hit me again so I have to kick him off and it starts to become a real fight – maybe this wasn't such a good idea. Why the fuck has this guy been cast? He can't act and he's already cost the production a lot of money by crashing into the wall of a house, nearly taking out the camera and crew in the process. So much for casting non-actors, I think, dodging the next few punches until Bent calls out 'Cut' and people drag the freak away. Still, it's exhilarating.

It's hard to hold anything against Bent for very long. He wrote this part for me. He's let me develop my own monologue in a key scene in the film. He's flown me here business class. He's given Bianca a job on the film, in publicity. He's given most people's partners jobs on the film, it's a family affair. It's also a Norwegian affair: a Norwegian film made in Spain. Norwegian wages are mixed with Spanish catering and culture. They serve wine with the meals, horrifying the Norwegian producer, but his Spanish counterpart told him no wine meant no crew. This is luxury filmmaking.

And on top of that, there's a sweet script, a fantastic role, and a two-bedroom apartment overlooking a beach in the Galician town of Panxon. Bent has asked me to help him out with directing Erik, the young man who plays the lead role, because it's Erik's first film and I'm a bit of a hero figure for him. We've had a deep discussion over the character Erik will play, and over Windy, the character I will play. Bent wants Windy to be larger than life. I want to be sure I don't overact. It's all so Professional.

And that's not all. This film is being taken seriously. It has attracted two of Spain's heavyweight actors, Pilar Bardem and Paco Rabal, legends of Spanish cinema. When Paco Rabal arrives, smoking, wheezing, coughing and hardly able to move because of his lungs, all the Spanish crew defers to him. The women massage him, the men get him brandy, cigars, coffee. There's a palpable respect in the air. When we film at an island lighthouse, trudging up a half-hour incline each day, Paco gets the forklift truck while we all get packs of equipment to carry. He can hardly act for lack of breath, he can hardly talk, but all the Spanish are in awe. This kind of respect could be my future. So I missed out on *Seven*. So what?

The production office is based in Vigo, a large port on the north-eastern coast said to be the main entry point for drugs into Europe. There is the old town where we do a lot of filming, all rustic if you ignore the mass of tourist trinket shops and the ubiquitous McDonald's. Then there is the town proper. A centre made up of clogged, thin, unplanned streets crammed with shops and supermarkets. Whole suburbs of high-rise, rust-stained flats stretching along the northern road out of town towards Santiago de Compostela, and the docklands where police and dockhands alike drive to work in Mercedes-Benzes and sports cars. There is an air of hidden, illicit decadence. Cafés and restaurants turn into salsa clubs after one a.m., all generations dancing together in a smog of marijuana smoke and suspicious queues for lavatory cubicles.

The pace is slower in Panxon. There's a church here, a cluster of flats, a few beach-side, family-run restaurants, a couple of shops. It's a fishing village with a sideline in holiday apartments. It's more my style. Each free day we have, Bianca and I breakfast downstairs with coffee and croissants, looking out over the Atlantic Ocean, or watching the TV that always has the sound turned down. Each day we join the film crew for a three-course lunch with wine while the cleaners set to work on the flat. We take a siesta along with the rest of the town, then go for a drive to the Portuguese border to look at relics, or inland to visit villages and drink coffee and cognac in their town squares.

We eat around ten p.m., and the locals start to prepare family dishes for us, serving homemade *Aguardiente de Hierbas* for us to drink because we are regulars. We promenade along the beach and watch the children playing and the teenagers preening and the parents fighting and the old couples remembering, before retiring to bed. When I walk on set I am fresh and rested and have ideas for scenes. Everyone commends my performance, laughs at my delivery, claps my little improvised dance scene. But something is wrong. Everyone else on set has rings under their eyes. Anita explains that it is hard for them, they are used to partying a lot because they take a two- to three-hour siesta in the middle of the day, and a couple of hours rest at night, but they can't take siestas on a film so sleep gets forgotten.

They are partying every night. I must be missing something. I want to know what.

One night a pyre of old junk is built on the beach, and a scarecrow figure full of fireworks is placed on top of it. The whole community comes out and sets it alight. Other fires can be seen on the beaches around. Anita tells us it is a ritual, to burn out the bad spirits of the year before and welcome the good spirits of the year to come. We should walk around the flames seven times anticlockwise and seven times clockwise. We do, despite the intense heat, and we are laughed at by the locals. Perhaps that's Anita's private joke. But I remember a friend from Sydney, a Jewish advocate of everything New Age, who told me that if I wished to be successful then I should act successful, that the Universal

Ether would recognise the trappings of success and treat me accordingly. Maybe, I start to think, she has a point. Maybe I should be reckless and confident instead of cautious and doubtful. The world helps those who help themselves! Let's follow the custom, joke or not, let's throw out the old spirits and bring in the new.

I've been sent a script by an American independent director, and I've been thinking I should just say yes. After all, who knows when the next opportunity to work will come? But it's a terrible script and it would be embarrassing to be seen in it and it doesn't pay much. Which is the more reckless approach? Which is the successful type of decision? To accept or reject? On the one hand, I get a trip to the States again, a bit of money, maybe meet people, take the risk of being seen in something that is woeful from inception, and be damned to the consequences. On the other, I say no to being in a piece of crap but run the risk of getting a reputation for being choosy as well as putting the director offside. God, even trying to be reckless is hard.

I reject the script. The director wants reasons. I give them. Now that's reckless! It's good. It feels like I am what people here are saying I am. Professional. Recklessly professional. Taking risks, like Windy's walk, like small roles, like saying no to bad work. I want more of it. I want to be wild as well as professional. I want to take chances with my personal and working life. Isn't that true creativity? All around me people are doing things that I'm not. Actors — partying, flirting, having affairs with the locals or else recounting all the affairs they have had, to anyone who will listen. Married crew members – out every night without their spouses; one even asked Bianca to have an affair with him, told her I wouldn't mind and his wife would be impressed. Unmarried crew members – having it off left, right and centre. It's an orgy out there, and I'm excluded. I need to find my inner Keith Richards, I need to live this life while I can. If I do, then either it will continue to come to me or else I won't regret not having done when it goes.

There is an end-of-week party at a crew member's place, a rambling house some way from Panxon along thin, winding dirt roads in the hills around the town. Bianca is the one who wants to leave. The party is fine but wouldn't I prefer to go home now, with her? I agree, but really I want to stay. One of the actors is in the corner with someone he's picked up. Anita is dancing samba with one of the grips. People are shouting, laughing, smoking, drinking. They can't believe we're going. Bianca is tipsy and acting seductively; there's sexual promise but I know she's holding me back. I get angrier and angrier but don't say a word. I don't want to go home, we go home all the time, I want to be OUT on my OWN. I want to be in the corner with a local or dancing samba with Anita or smoking, drinking, laughing, shouting. I want to be reckless and cool and totally, utterly desired by the world, like Erik, like Paco. I wait until we get back.

'Look, I didn't really want to leave,' I say. 'I'm going to drive back.'

She's a bit shocked. 'What? Why didn't you just say?'

'Well, I was thinking of you. You wanted to go. I didn't want to hurt your feelings.'

She looks at me. 'Are you joking?' she asks.

I shake my head. 'So now I've got you home, I'm thinking of me, okay? And I'm going back.'

'Nicholas,' she says, 'we were going to spend the night together, you said you wanted to as well . . . I thought to just be together –'

'Yeah well,' I interrupt, 'I changed my mind. I was having fun.'

Her eyes have gone bloodshot, but it's too late to back out now.

'Nicholas, you didn't mention this before. I had no idea you wanted to stay. And you've drunk too much. You shouldn't be driving. You've got no sense of direction. You'll get lost.'

'I've got a map,' I say.

She closes her eyes and takes a breath. I wonder if she'll break.

'You do remember we had arrangements for tomorrow, don't you? If you go back you're going to be too tired.'

I stay mute. I'm waiting for her to get out. Her voice goes steely.

'Don't go. You'll ruin tonight, you'll ruin tomorrow. You may ruin a lot more. There's something else going on here.'

'Fuck that,' I say, 'I'm going. Are you getting out?'

She slams the door as she leaves. She's really angry now. She stands screaming in the middle of the road as I drive away.

'Fuck you, you self-obsessed bastard, why can't you . . .'

I do my best to ignore it. Whatever I do is going to be as bad so I may as well just go. And anyway, this is *my* film, *my* part, *my* crew, and I'm going to hang out with them just for once, and I'm glad she's going home. I want to spend all night partying with work mates. I want to flirt. Maybe I'll pick someone up, who knows, it can't cause any further damage, and fuck it I'm semi-famous, it's my due! I want to be what everyone says actors are. I want people to get drunk and tell me how good I am. I want to be selfish, I want to do it by myself. I may never be one of the lead actors in a film again! I may never work in Spain again. I should indulge!

Annoyingly, Bianca's right. I get lost on the way. When I arrive, the party is packing up. It's been very sedate. I hang around a while. There's no drinking, no flirting. Now I'm here, I don't actually want to be.

Some people are going on to another party, but I'm too tired to be bothered. I can't think of anything that'd be likely to happen at the next party that would make further tiredness worthwhile. I wonder if maybe I just don't have an inner Keith Richards. I wonder if it matters. I wonder whose expectations I want to live up to – mine, the media's, some amorphous Other's. I wonder if the Ether will be disappointed. I wonder if I have what it takes to be a wild success.

When I get home Bianca is furious. 'I hope the party was worth it,' she bites.

'It was finished,' I answer, hoping she'll laugh. She doesn't. I try to act normal. I even forget that we've fought – I was drunk, I tell myself, it was in a haze, it wasn't what I thought. There was no orgy. No wild excess. No un-divided, exotic, erotic, ecstatic, illicit attention. It doesn't count.

It's not that easy. Bianca still acts hurt. There's unfin-ished business, and I don't know how to fix it. It doesn't seem enough to try to explain that you thought you wanted someone else's life, then found out that maybe you didn't.

CHAPTER 7

the meaning of life

The Accountants, Adelaide, 1977

My family moved to Elizabeth. I went with them.

Elizabeth, it turned out, was a failed industrial satellite town to the north of Adelaide. Full of disenfranchised English migrants, an up-market form of Whyalla. They all worked at the local GMH car plant, which was in trouble, or at the Levi's factory, which wasn't. The kids fancied themselves as British skinheads and would go to Adelaide on the train each Friday night to have fights with the Hindley Street Rockers, because the Hindley Street Rockers were wogs.

I missed the bush, but Adelaide on the horizon was an exciting city. There were old hippies there, men with long, lank hair and women in loose cheesecloth blouses, who had nothing to do with the skinheads and the rockers and the violence. There was the Festival Theatre, where concerts and plays were held. There was the River Torrens, where willow trees swept into the water and paddleboats could be hired. There were pubs where bands played and people danced and talked and didn't fight. There were vineyards in driving distance, and hills with European-style towns like Hahndorf, settled by old German migrants.

Then punk rock dribbled on to the Australian scene, two years late. I'd met a few other kids who wanted to watch bands. We'd take the bus for an hour into Adelaide – it was safer than the train – to watch leather-clad, skinny boys with eye make-up doing Iggy Pop songs at the university bar. We didn't know that they were Iggy Pop songs. It was new and fresh and rebellious and exciting, it was raw, it wasn't disco, it wasn't Elizabeth, it was in the university bar, for God's sake, the audience was educated. Most of the new friends had that Elizabeth, fake-skinhead past, prided themselves on being tough, still thought fart jokes funny, were homophobic and racist by default. They weren't what I thought might be my type, but they'd have to do. They were the only people I knew and they were my ticket into this fresh new world.

We started a band. At 25, Ben was the eldest. He was a clerk in the births and deaths registration department, and believed himself to be a Neo-Nazi, though he didn't know the word 'neo' then. Ben wore swastikas in his time off and claimed to hate Jews, even though he'd never met any, but dropped it all after the TV series 'Holocaust'. He hadn't realised about the death camps, he said. What a tosser, I thought, but the others wanted him in the band, and I suspected they'd choose him over me, so I didn't say.

At 16, Laurence was the youngest. He was the son of a radical feminist poet, and was still at school, whereas Sean, Pete and I were 18, unemployed, and living with our parents in Elizabeth. Laurence was the only one who could play. The rest of us chose our instruments by what we could get cheap. My cousin from the UK, newly arrived and depressed in Whyalla, had a bass guitar I could have for $20. Sean had access to a drum kit with no bass drum. Ben the tosser had an electric that he couldn't play. Pete had fat fingers so he had to sing. When the bass guitar arrived it only had four strings. I was shocked, but it made it easier to learn. I was stunned to find out you needed an amplifier as well.

Punk rock made it easy to form a band, and there was nothing like being in a band to justify strutting. Five egos, someone called us. It took months to learn a few songs. It was my job to copy the bass lines from records and make the others follow on the guitar. 'You Really Got Me', 'Louie Louie', 'I Can't Explain' – but that one minus the chorus 'cos the chords changed too much for Ben the tosser to follow. Typical. The others were more into posing, which is why it took so long, even in the bloody rehearsal room where there was no one but themselves to pose to. And we were paying for this, we were renting the rehearsal room. I had to shout at them each week just to get them to play together or try to. They just wanted to bang on their instruments, make disconnected noise, individual wanking. At this rate we'd never get out of the rehearsal room. They'd all just drown in their own impotent ego semen and take me with them. It was exhausting. I knew if we ever did anything, if we ever played together, if we ever got on a stage, it would be 'cos of me.

And we did. Punk was hip. We kids nearly even dressed right. Torn T-shirts, leather jackets, tight torn jeans, pins, ripped logos, pouting mouths, uncontrollable feedback. We called ourselves The Accountants. We caused a storm. The worst thing we could've done was learn to play, but there was no chance of that. We were so incompetent we needed people to tune our guitars for us, so drunk we got fans to hold us up while we played, so full of ourselves we thought we were the best band in town and resented everyone else. Parties got held in our honour, girls crawled through the windows of packed rooms just to get the chance of sleeping with us, older women queued up to get a go with Laurence, now called Jonny in honour of Rotten.

It was terrifying.

I was unadmittedly, shamefully virginal. Full of performance anxiety and Catholic guilt. Desperate to get laid but wouldn't come across. It made me an enigma, which I loved, but fucking hell it was frustrating, I was missing my chance. All the parties were in Adelaide and one of the groupies had a swimming pool in the hills. Girls would jump in topless while older men would sit on the poolside and offer them drugs. Maybe that's the way, I thought, but topless girls, intimidating dealers were too, too threatening.

Still, we were the darlings of the punk scene. The Marryatville Hotel in one of the richer suburbs of Adelaide was our haunt. We'd drive there from Elizabeth every Friday night to play, or else to watch other, lesser bands. Our fans knew we'd be there. We gloried in it. Then one night a huge fight broke out, a bikie gang got in. They sat me on a billiard table, then lined up to take turns at headbutting me. I was in shock, I could see it happening, but couldn't even think to raise my hands to protect my face. I was just surprised I couldn't feel anything. This girl who'd been trying to lay me – and I'd been thinking maybe I should take the plunge, face the risk of being shamed – managed to drag me into the girls' toilets, told me not to look in the mirror, she'd arrange an ambulance. The bikies were clamouring at the door when she ran out, but they wouldn't come in, only poofters would go in the girls' loo. The first thing I did was look in the mirror. My front teeth were missing, but maybe that was them sticking out of the lip which was dangling by a thread, swinging as I trembled. I hadn't realised I was trembling. I couldn't see a nose, just a jelly-like thing spread over the face. The eyes were disappearing behind bruises. I couldn't really recognise myself in the reflection. It was fascinating.

I looked pretty tough for a while there, all scars, bandages and bruises, but I didn't feel it. My nose was packed with cotton wool, my lips were full of stitches, and my front teeth were ceramic. The fascination faded quickly. But then I met this girl – woman, really – older than me, multi-coloured hair, just back from London, all punk clothes and cockney accent and terribly, terribly interested in me, even with the bandages and flattened nose. She wanted to be a singer and I was such a good bass player and I knew what life was about. I'd had it rough, she could tell. There was a small problem, an addiction – heroin – but she was getting over it. Anyway, it wasn't a problem if you knew how to handle it, but she was sick of working at the strip club to pay for it. Did I want to come and see her work?

She needed a knight in shining armour to help her, I could tell, and I needed an older, experienced, street-wise and maybe just slightly drugged – at least the first time round – woman, and just imagine, we could help each other, and it'd be great. I'd have left the suburbs behind, I'd be in a new band, I'd be respected and loved and sexed and talented like I always knew I would. It was all just waiting. The world would be our oyster, all the untouched groupies agreed, there would be record companies banging on the door.

We moved into a house in Elizabeth. It was cheaper there. I began work at the post office.

Drug dealers drove up from Adelaide to do deals with the punk woman. They were the only people banging on the door, at all hours.

It just wasn't what I'd imagined.

London, winter 1998

Bianca and I go to London. We've got money from Spain so we can give it a try. It would be silly not to, after all I've just been in two major films. Work breeds work. And it's close to Oslo. Bianca's getting job offers there now. Maybe we can commute.

We move into a shared house in Kilburn. Wallpaper peeling, stairs buckling, telephone booths overflowing with prostitutes' cards. Streets filled with the same chain shops arranged in the same order. Homeless people in cardboard boxes and sleeping bags, trying to doze in doorways or under bridges. Buskers being chased out of the tube by police. Drunk boys and men spilling on to the pavement after the pubs' eleven p.m. closing time, screaming sexual abuse and football slogans at passers-by. Rents more than a full week's income on the minimum wage. Tony Blair's faux-social-work marshmallow sincerity bleating on TV about the socio-political New Labour force of New Britain. Plans for an unrivalled Millennium Dome to put London back on the map. Grey, heavy clouds pressing. The economy booming.

A move to a small flat in Westbourne Park. The floor sloping so much that telephone books get put under the sofa's front legs to even it out. The bathroom an add-on, carved out of the living space. Carpeted and unsealed, any splashed water from the shower leaking through the floor on to the electricity meters down in the hallway. The flat shaking with so much traffic noise you have to shout to be heard. A steal at £170 a week unfurnished. The others in the block are paying £250.

Lots of auditions. Producers running out halfway through because someone has just stolen their motorbike helmet, directors musing aloud whether you can lose your obviously Dutch accent, casting agents wanting to know if you've ever been on 'Neighbours'. Some work. A priest in a film in Yorkshire where one of the local extras keeps telling you about her friend who had to turn down the part because of dates, but who would have been much better than you. A Czech psychotic in a BBC telemovie that gets lots of interest, but everybody thinks you are actually Czech and there aren't many roles for Czech actors in London. A guest role as a Czech scientist in a cheap commercial police series. Several months in a call centre for charities, £5 an hour and warning pips if you spend too long on any one call.

My agent says to be patient, careers take time to evolve, especially for character actors. 'I'm 39 years old,' I tell her. 'How much more patient do I have to be?'

'Just hang in there,' she replies with a smile. 'There won't be many character actors your age left in another ten years – you'll corner the market.'

Ten years. She means ten years in London. I'm not sure I can handle another day.

Riga, spring 1998

And then suddenly I'm drunk in the studio in Riga, Latvia, and it's more than I ever imagined. God, it's miles and smiles from both Whyalla and London. And I am everybody's darling and I don't really truly know how I got here, I just need another drink, more compliments. Surely there's a party somewhere, this may not be Hollywood but there's some kind of celebrity rock'n'roll movie-star ethic going on, I am head of it and so I should be! Ever since the opening of the telephone box and the wax Eisenstein, the Riga Film Festival has continued in surreal bliss. *Bad Boy Bubby* has been, as always, a popular favourite. I have been swamped with admirers on the streets and in the bars and at the parties. The Vodka Vampires, women on mini-stilts in sci-fi suits with tanks of vodka on their backs and vodka pistol siphons in their hands, have kept my glass permanently filled at official functions. I have been the official guest of the Australian and French embassies. I have judged the Celebrity Haircutting Competition. I have been installed outside cinemas that aren't even showing my film to sign autographs. I have been rescued by journalists and festival staff from a gang-fan attack. I haven't paid for anything. I am King. Was there ever any doubt?

Riga is fabulous, an injection, the promise of what could be, the Eastern European version of glamour. My Hollywood. The city centre is being rebuilt to mirror what it was like before World War II. It is beautiful: all pristine cathedrals and renovated fairytale buildings. On the outskirts of the central business district there are several zeppelin hangars built by a forward-thinking council to anticipate the huge business that zeppelin air travel would bring. They are being used as markets. Meat, fish, vegetables, clothes, hardware. Lining the streets outside the hangars are the traders who can't afford stalls inside, and patrolling them are the police. This reborn city is going to be law-abiding.

A few streets further on the city turns feral, the past in the present. Buildings still have holes from where bombs have hit, windows are broken, roads pitted. Prostitutes line the streets at night. The Lenin Café is near the crossover to this section. It is unchanged since the days of the Soviets except anti-communist graffiti has been added to communist graffiti on the walls, alongside posters of Lenin and Marx and the hammer and sickle. It serves one style of beer and has a continuous pot of brewed tea. There is a small selection of Latvian cakes in a cracked container. I love this café, it appears so chic, but the lights of the centre look so much brighter, so much newer, so filled with carbonated, sugary promise. Back there, at the central fountain in the town square each Friday at six p.m., young men congregate with posies of flowers, waiting for their dates. A couple of streets away the Swingers Club operates for crowds of sexually liberated and hungry youth. There is an air of near-hysterical optimism. The city is hungry, the bright lights look new, and for now I'm King.

I attend the festival prize-giving ceremony, an Irish Coffee Lottery. Thirteen films – a selection of comedies, dramas, documentaries and shorts – are up for the US$10,000 best film prize. Everyone gets a cup of Irish coffee. The filmmaker who finds the festival director's button in their coffee wins. A Canadian documentary maker swallows, squeals with excitement, and chokes on the button. Fireworks go off, the trees in the courtyard catch alight, some men leap on stage and demolish a cast-iron sculpture with a blowtorch and chainsaw. They extract a gold ingot and give it to her. The crowd goes wild. The ingot-holding Canadian documentary maker is swamped. The Vodka Vampires reappear. It's all too much, I can't bear to watch it end. I go back to the hotel.

I am at the bar. The festival bar. With a pretty Russian teenager half my age. I was talking to a French filmmaker when he saw two girls being turned away for not having a festival pass. He ran over and ushered them in. A blonde and a brunette.

The filmmaker asked if I would mind looking after the brunette, talk to her or something while he took the blonde away for a while. He winked as he asked. He didn't wait for a reply.

I check with the Russian whether she thinks her friend minds going for a walk. 'Oh yes,' she replies, 'he buys her drinks.' So I buy her one. It seems only polite. 'Double vodka and tonic,' she says.

The Russian tells me she doesn't know what to expect. This may be her last week in Riga. She doesn't have much money. She must take life as it comes. Riga is building up to a referendum on the status of the Russian population in

Latvia, whether they should be allowed citizenship or not. Most of the Russians can't speak Latvian, they've been here as members of an oppressive Soviet regime. Now the Latvians want revenge. If the vote goes against the Russians, most will have to move back to Russia. They will not be allowed to take their belongings. She will be penniless.

I don't know what to say.

'You are an older man,' she says, breaking the silence. 'Tell me please, for you, after experience, what is the meaning of life?'

I answer as best I can. 'Love,' I tell her. 'I think that's as much as you can hope for.'

She doesn't react. Just sips her drink. Then she tells me her parents have lived in Riga for most of her life, to stay in this hotel has been one of their holiday ambitions never realised. Now she has the chance to see what it is like. Would I show her my room?

How can I refuse?

She sighs when she walks in and looks around. 'It is not so grand,' she says. English is not her first language, but the disappointment registers strong. She takes off her coat. The dress underneath is sheer and flimsy. She moves to the bed, stretches herself out on it. She is very pretty.

I remain standing in the doorway. I don't let the door shut. These moments, I've never really known how to conduct them. It should be easy, this is a famous actor's perk. It goes with the rest of what's been happening here. I may never be King again. It's a second chance, maybe a last chance, to indulge. And no one is watching. I would hate to think of Bianca even considering what I'm considering. But if no one knows . . .

She turns and tilts her head to look out the window, baring her neck, and raises one knee so the dress slides up a little.

I have never liked the classic signs of physical flirtation. Coming as they do with feigned intellectual denial. In one so young it is painful to see. And she hasn't seen the film. She doesn't even know I'm an actor. She just knows I'm from the West. This isn't even an actor's perk.

'Your friend may be back,' I say. She makes no comment, swings her legs off the bed, takes her glass and coat. We leave the room. She looks with interest at the 1970s furnishings in the hallway. We don't speak.

Downstairs, the French filmmaker is trying to put his arm around the blonde's shoulders and she is shrugging him off gently. He has bought her another drink and is looking frustrated. 'We're going to a nightclub,' he tells me. 'Would you like to come?'

'Not me,' I say. 'I've got an early flight.'

'But it's the last night of the festival,' says the Frenchman.

The blonde talks quickly to the Russian in Russian. 'I will come if my friend can come,' says the blonde.

'Both of you?' says the Frenchman. I am forgotten. He orders her another drink.

I can't take any more. I feel like the military on R&R. I go upstairs and pack. I put all the clothes I have brought with me, all the new, fashionable items from sales in New London, all the New Me, into the new, hard, powder-blue suitcase, and shut them inside.

Berlevåg, winter 1999

It is close to the return of the sun in Berlevåg, northern Norway, the beginning of the change of season that goes from 24-hour darkness to 24-hour light, and people are celebrating. On the weekends, the main street is full of drunk locals dressed in bright red and yellow quilted jump-suits, struggling like newly born deer not to slip on the ice. Cars and trucks sit outside the three pubs, engines constantly running to stop them from freezing. There are bingo mornings and singalong nights. There is a wet T-shirt competition. The women keep their bras on and use heated water, because of the cold. There is a community dance in the town hall. People bring their own Coke bottles filled with home-burnt, self-made alcohol that tastes like methylated spirits and is added to anything drinkable. Coffee, Coke, lemonade, tea. People fall over in corners. The local hot-dog store man goes home and beats up his wife for sleeping, then beats up his mother-in-law for inter-vening. 'You have to be tough to live in Berlevåg,' explains his friend.

Before I came here, I met with Toni Collette in London. The same year that I had won the AFI for best actor, she had won the AFI for best actress. She was off to Hollywood to work on some huge film with Bruce Willis. Where on earth, she asked me, is Berlevåg?

It is a small town, situated on the coast of the Barents Sea, on one of the northernmost tips of Norway near the border of Sweden and Russia. There's one main road with a few tributary streets radiating out. The houses – brightly coloured red, yellow and blue wooden structures – hold grimly on to the ice. Some have already disintegrated, and the rotten beams stick out of the snow, all forlorn and abandoned. There are some shops at the end of the road, and a community hall shows films once a week. A long jetty leads out to sea, forming a man-made harbour that allows fishing boats and ferries to shelter from the storms and high tides that batter the coast. The jetty is packed tight with two-metre-tall concrete tetrapods, like giant prickles.

I am here for a film about corruption in the cod fishing industry, directed by Knut Erik Jensen. I met him in Tromsø and he's brought me over from London to play a Norwegian fish-factory caretaker with a speech impediment. Cerebral palsy of the vocal cords. The character doesn't say much, but he's around a lot. The speech impediment has been invented so that I can play the part. 'I knew we would work together one day!' Knut Erik says.

He is filming only what he needs for the edit. Every shot has been pre-planned and drawn in a story-board book that comes with the script. We sometimes film half scenes without the other characters because it is more camera-efficient, the first assistant director reading out their lines to give me something to respond to.

In between shots Knut Erik tells stories about how his first film nearly didn't get made because one of the investors was wavering. He was put off by the fact that the whole thing was going to be shot as a single, long, slow-motion flashback with only one spoken line. Knut Erik stormed into the man's office and began to pull it apart, shouting at him that he did not have the power to stop this film. 'It worked, Nicholas,' says Knut Erik. 'The money was signed off the next morning.'

Knut Erik is in love with the far north of the country: the people, the landscape, the history. He wants most of his films to be about it. He has, he believes, the chance to make seven more films before he dies if he keeps on at the same rate. He knows what most of them will be. There is another role for me in there, an English sea captain just after the war years, doing the crossover from Scotland to Finnmark, who gets involved with the local girls but never stays. It is a story about growing up as a young boy in the post-war years, the first signs of desire felt in the dancing lessons with the local big-breasted dancing teacher who would hug the young boys' heads into her cleavage as they practised the Vienna Waltz. It's all there in his head – he has built up the crew and the actors he likes to work with. Most of them are here now, they are close, they work well together, they are a family of sorts. I could be part of it.

The lead actor has worked once before with Knut Erik, in a film with the lead actress, but this time he's apprehensive. 'Knut Erik isn't listening to anyone any more,' he tells me. 'He thinks he is king, he thinks we are cattle.' He continues, 'I'm so glad you're in this. You're a real actor, not like some of the others.' He explains he is proud of his success, he wasn't born into an acting family like other Norwegian actors, he trained as a chef, his father was a well-known singer and his mother the accompanist. It was a lonely ride to the top.

The lead actress uses the American Method technique. I have a day off, but she requests that I sit out of sight in the bedroom of the house she is filming in because in this particular scene, the caretaker is supposed to be asleep in there. As a Method actor she needs to feel that the scene is as close to reality as possible. The first assistant director opens the window so I can sneak out if I want, but she checks after each take to make sure I'm still there. She doesn't mind that I read, just having me in there is enough. The lead actor can't stand it.

The make-up man recognises another non-Norwegian to confide in. He talks in a quiet, serious voice, and takes time from applying make-up to look into my eyes. He is Swedish. He finds many things about Norwegian habits and culture exasperating and backward. The lack of supplied school lunches, the arrangement of meals, the lack of precision in jewellery making. Much of this reflects in the other crew members, whose experience and professionalism do not match his. This is to do with their Norwegianness. There has been no Norwegian Bergman, and it shows.

The Swedish chef invites me to come with him over the border to Finland where he can buy cheaper, better quality food and smuggle it back. He's a fan of *Bubby* and can't believe the lead actor is in this film. He says it's one of the reasons he accepted the job, he wants to get to know me as a kind of pay-off. I am his cult-celebrity bonus.

I accept. I want to join the family.

The supermarket is about three kilometres inside the Finnish border. It stands totally on its own, with nothing else man-made around, and it is full. It is there to cater for people willing to run the gauntlet of smuggling food past the border guards. Every now and again, the guards stop a car and prosecute the owner, but it's worth the risk. The food is a third of the price and much better.

On the way back, the chef points to a blue house on the outskirts of a town that is just inside the Russian border. 'That's the Russian prostitutes' house,' he explains. 'A Norwegian man bought it, and every weekend he gets a posse of young Russian prostitutes to stay there. You can visit them in the house, or you can go and select one and pay for them to come back home with you for the weekend.'

'Berlevåg's population grows on the weekends,' he continues. 'A lot of the men like the Russian girls – they can't speak Norwegian. It's causing a lot of marriage problems. The women in Berlevåg and surrounding towns have tried to close it down. The men won't marry them if they can pay such cheap rates for sex. The councils haven't closed it down, but they are trying to get the prices up to Norwegian rather than Russian rates, to make it less attractive. It's difficult, though. Prostitution isn't legal so it's hard to define an official rate. Would you like to go for a visit?'

At night, the male choir practises in the pub below my room. The first time I watch, one of them dares me to go deer hunting with him on the weekend. Before I can answer he starts to *joik* in my face. He is a Sami, he explains.

'I'd love to,' I tell him during a pause in his singing, 'but I don't think I could kill the deer.'

'But you eat it, city boy!' he answers, staring into my eyes, and begins to *joik* again.

An Indian man who is playing pool saves me by challenging me to a game. He looks out of place here in the icy north. I ask him why he chose to come to Berlevåg.

'I work in the fish factory,' he replies. 'Good money, good people. Good lifestyle. The people here, they are not racist, you know? Not like elsewhere. There is no racism.'

'That's great,' I say.

'Yes,' he replies, 'they are not racist because I am a Sikh. I work hard, you know? I am no lazy Paki shit!'

Even though it is nearing the end of winter, Berlevåg is still frozen solid and buffeted by snowstorms. The average temperature is around minus ten if you ignore the wind-chill factor. The light is constantly blue. The sun lies below the horizon most of the day, so light is refracted upwards. Daytime is a constant twilight. The sky is the same colour and texture as the ground, distorting perspective and balance. Russian fishing boats, their hulls pure rust, are docked in the tiny harbour, frozen washing strung out on lines across the decks. The boats are impounded because the Russian shipping company hasn't paid the harbour taxes. The crews haven't been paid, either.

The graveyard is some kilometres away. There is an old one near the Lutheran church, by the hill that kids toboggan down, but it's no longer used because the ground stays frozen with permafrost. Gravediggers couldn't get deep enough so the bodies lay close to the surface and froze, only beginning to rot in summer as they thawed out. It created an odour problem that made it even harder to be here.

Everything looks impermanent apart from the ice. Civilisation is losing. There are no McDonald's, no Hungry Jack's, no Kentucky Frieds, no Pizza Huts. No Coles or Woolworths or Kmarts. Television shows an alien world with bizarre, alien rules – 'Ally McBeal', 'Friends', 'Letterman', 'Oprah'. They have no context out here in the ice. There is a constant disintegration of human endeavour. It is oddly comforting.

Our crew has started to form a community with the hotel staff and the locals. The film unit decides to pay for a prawn dinner and a disco as an offer of thanks to the town. People sit around drinking beer and shelling buckets of prawns while the two-man-travelling-disco team set up their equipment and begin to play their CDs. It's a full moon outside and the snow is providing a reflective backdrop through the wall-length window behind them. Johnny Cash and Abba take turns to squeal through the tinny speakers, and crew members and locals dance uncomfortably together. In between songs the low *rrrrrrrrrrrr* of the car engines can be heard, and outside the door there's a haze of car fumes. By three a.m. everyone is drunk and the home-burnt alcohol is on the tables. Bianca, shouting over the traffic on the phone from the flat in London, has warned me never to drink home-burnt, she says it's virtually poisonous, I wouldn't survive. I haven't, but everyone else has and it shows. The discomfort has gone, but the pub is closing and the party spills over into Knut Erik's apartment. He sits at the kitchen table, blearily admiring a stereotypical Scandinavian woman. Big breasts, big blonde hair. She says she has two children to go home to but doesn't move. He takes hold of her hair, asks me to admire it, feel its weight, feel its voluptuousness. She waits patiently for me to do so, smiling at us both while I bounce her hair in my hands. She's still there when I leave at five a.m. The boundaries are broken. From then on, we are greeted on the street.

The lead actress, the first assistant director, the runner and the assistant make-up girl all agree to be in a short film I make on the weekend on a mini digital video camera. The landscape is too good not to use. I've never made a film before and I fuss over every set-up, but they stay with me in freezing temperatures and we complete the thing. I forget about sound so it is unusable. The actors are aghast but polite. Still, I sit in my room the next day and replay the images over and over, surprised I have been able to create something so quickly and easily.

I go that night to do my speech-impediment part in the lead actress's next big Method scene, where she plunges into the sea, gets hauled out, stripped naked and wrapped in blankets, all in minus 20 degrees Celsius temperatures. My job is to drive the dinghy it all happens in. We shoot it three times, in the sea. By the end she is turning blue and screaming with cramp and cold. It looks very real. It is very real.

The next night I am back in the rubber dinghy. It is my last shot. I have to chase a Russian trawler and rescue the lead actress when she jumps off it into the sea. The water is crystal calm. I look like the Michelin man, clad in five layers of alternating wool and rubber, and I am roasting despite the minus 30 degrees Celsius temperature with windchill factor. The air is so cold it's hard to breathe.

We go out beyond the harbour, and the water snap-freezes when it splashes. I get hit by tiny globules of ice. A seal surfaces a few metres away, looking at us. The camera crew is in a dinghy behind me, waiting for the rusting Russian trawler to get into position. It should be the first wages the crew has made in months, but the rumour is that the Russian company has diverted the money into the harbour taxes. Everything is quiet apart from the lapping waves. The air is icy clean. It is hypnotic.

Someone yells out, 'Nicholas! Look up!' I do. The sky is dancing. It's the first time I have seen the Northern Lights, and they are huge. The whole of the night sky is a swirling mass of luminescent silver. It looks alive. Maybe I'm on drugs, I think fleetingly. This has to be the best Actor's Perk yet. Then the trawler gets into place and Knut Erik yells 'Action!' in English for me, and I skim across the waves in the middle of the night in the Barents Sea with the Northern Lights overhead and the sea spitting up ice below, a rusting Russian trawler in front and a camera crew chasing behind.

I used to be a bank clerk in Whyalla, I think to myself.

Sydney, spring 1999

A young man at the airport has a sign with my name written on it. He recognises me before I see it and comes over with his hand stretched out. 'Gdaiaiemjrrff?' he asks. There are very few pronounced vowels and only the odd recognisable consonant. He is young and holding a mini-ature scooter under one arm, so I don't know if this is a joke or some sort of new slang I'm not up to date with. 'Sorry?' I reply. It is hard to think of anything else after 26 hours on an economy flight from London with the knowledge that you're expected to be in rehearsals in the next few hours. He slows it down. 'G'day. Iem Jeoff?' Shit, I think, it's just the accent, I'd forgotten how stridently unformed it makes the language sound.

'Hi, I'm Nicholas,' I answer, a bit unnecessarily, after all he is carrying a piece of cardboard with my name scrawled on it. 'Yehieneeow? Iseeryuhinberdboibubbie? Grousemovie-meneh?' This is too hard. 'I'm really sorry, could you speak a bit slower, I'm very jet-lagged,' I explain. Jeff understands. He lives an hour away from the airport, he's had to get up at five a.m. to pick me up. Man, is he tired! I owe him for getting up so early! Yeah man, five a.m., what kind of time is that?

I look at him. He is getting uglier by the minute. Jeff shepherds me to a car. He's going to drive me to my accom-modation so I can shower and then go for the medical and then go straight to rehearsals. He drives very fast and talks to me all the way except when he's on the mobile. He's made short films – well, he's going to. Do I do short films? Maybe he could show me the script, there's a part in there . . .

Sydney looks glorious out of the window. The sun is out and the city shimmers in comparison with London. Everything is bright: the water of the harbour as we go over the Harbour Bridge is as blue as blue as blue, the Opera House shells look wonderfully eccentric, even the corporate high-rise façade of North Sydney glitters . . .

'So've you done much since *Bad Boy Bubby*, shit man that was grouse, I mean this is a small part, right, it's not the lead, right, so've you done any other leads? – Yeah, babe, I'm on my way. What, what, cian't hear ya, ya breakin up, nah, nah, I'll be there soon. He's fiene. Yeah, got up at five a.m. Man, what kind of time . . .'

The apartment looks out over the water. I can't wait to shower and just lie down for half an hour. Jeff sits in the armchair. 'Ayell wait for you to have a shower then we'll go to the dokta?' It is seven-thirty a.m. I can't believe the doctor's surgery will be open, and I've just been on a plane for 26 hours. But Jeff reassures me, 'Nah, it's okay, they made a speashal arrangement? The surgery is opening early just for us?'

There is no room to undress in the bathroom. I start stripping off right in front of him. He just turns his back. I want to break his neck.

At the office I meet the production crew and mention that I haven't been able to even lie down yet, my back is killing me. 'That's right,' says one of them, 'we thought it'd be better if you didn't sleep before the rehearsal.' I don't say anything. My brain is still fudgy from the travel. But I'm thinking, who the fuck came up with that bit of logic?

Rehearsals are tense. Clara, the director, is Chinese. The lead actor is Japanese. 'There's a cultural issue,' the dodgy production man tells me, 'a China/Japan thing. Might be a gender one, too, I dunno. But you'll be right.'

The Japanese male lead won't look at Clara. This might be because he is concentrating on his interpreter, and trying to explain why he disagrees with everything Clara says. Translation appears to be difficult. Clara asks me to give my feedback on acting and the role for him since it's his first feature film. I may be able to clarify certain things, I have had experience and training. It's a male-to-male ploy, and I feel sympathetic, but I just want to go to bed. We labour through until six p.m.

I can't sleep. I wander round to the nearest pub. It's full of people in white shirts and ties, or black skirts with thigh slits in them and low-cut tops. They all speak like Jeff and they are all Caucasian. The shirts are whiter and stiffer than those I remember from London, and they cover more flesh. There is more flesh to cover. Beer bellies poke out over belts, buttocks crinkle into pleated cushions. Maybe it's just the end of the day, lack of sleep, too much Jeff, but it just seems obscene. Suddenly I feel like I'm back at the bank's bash. I phone Bianca. She's packed up the London flat and is working in Oslo for a while, then she's going to join me in Sydney. I'm not sure she should. I'm not sure I want to be here. Maybe I want to be in sub-zero Oslo, cooking dinner and waiting for her to come home.

'Don't worry,' she says, looking out from her office at Norsk Film over the austere glint of Oslo ice, 'it'll pass.'

Lightning Ridge, spring 1999

And of course she is right. A few days later we all fly out to Lightning Ridge, an opal-mining town. It's hard to imagine. One main street with a few tributaries branching off, in the middle of otherwise uninhabited land. The polar opposite of Berlevåg. No defined population. Too many of them are avoiding the tax office or the law. Few people admit to a surname. If you went missing here no one would know.

The supermarkets are full of high-quality goods. Rows of vegetables, trucked in from down south. A wide choice of tinned and packaged foods, of cleaning agents, toothpastes, toilet rolls, the lot. The community centre is full of equipment. The pub is ultra-suburban with wide-screen TV, boutique beers, an extensive range of spirits and wine, a shaded patio area with barbecue. Enough people make enough money to afford all this. Lightning Ridge is a rich opal-mining town.

The mines are human termites' nests, wide vistas of white clay craters dotting the landscape. Bits of scrub survive on the yellowy-red dust in between. There are shantytown dwellings of corrugated iron and remodelled cars, all built on a cliff-edge plateau looking out across an endless plain of low, densely packed trees. Storms linger out there and lightning flickers on the horizon, giving the town its name. Sometimes the storms rage over the plateau, ripping up plants and loose dwellings and turning the dust, clay and craters to mulch in minutes. The storms pass over, circle around and charge in again. It's an unbelievably filmic landscape. The outskirts of the earth.

The townsfolk are on our side. We have locals working on crew. They've helped build the church that features in the film, with only one minor incident. One of the builders was going too slow and the boss smashed his head into the ground four times. Told him he was sick of his junkie habits, to get lost and not come back. The guy ran off and the boss sent everyone home. 'Don't come back until tomorrow,' he said. 'The guy's a junkie but he collects guns.'

One of the crew says there's a town about three hours south where every shop is boarded up and the pub sells T-shirts with the logo: 'I stopped in Walgett and lived.' The police won't go there.

So I've been warned: don't tell ANYONE that you're playing an incestuous paedophile unless you want to be killed. There's a lot of empty mines out there, and no one knows how many bodies are down them.

That's right, incestuous paedophile. I have been flown to Lightning Ridge from London to play an incestuous paedophile in an Australian film about a blind girl's trip across New South Wales to take revenge on her incestuous grandfather who is also her father. It is, in its way, a beautiful script, with an interesting part, an exciting director. I nearly missed out because the stand-in casting agent thought I only did psychopaths, and incestuous paedophile didn't quite fit the mark. I'm confused. So far as I know I've only played one psychopath and that was on British TV. Tortured, innocent eccentric is more how I see the pattern, which is why this role is of interest. This guy, who is 30 at the beginning of the film and 70 by the end, goes mad with the knowledge of what he's done. It's a stretch on all counts, physically, mentally and morally. But not a stretch of the type the stand-in casting agent thought. And I'm getting paid $25,000. How could I say no?

It's an odd place to be. On the fringes of the globe again, in startling heat, playing someone who will be seen as inherently evil. Girlfriend on the very opposite of the world, in ice-bound Oslo, writing scripts. Violent people with guns around. A weird kind of splendid desolation populated by brutish barbarism. A supposedly glamorous job in an intensely magnified Whyalla.

Somewhere along the line those heady moments in Venice have translated to this.

I'm the only one who is having a good time with the director. The lead actress is young and physically very slight. She needs attention that isn't coming, and she can't do anger without bursting into tears. She's crying a lot. The lead Japanese actor has lost his interpreter and is overwhelmed by flies that make him feel dirty. He is developing a nervous hand flick to deal with them. Other actors are questioning the lack of safety footage, the stylisation, the required precision, the lack of close-ups. One of the child actresses has her whole family with her. The parents are worried about how successful the film will be. They haven't read the script, but it doesn't look very commercial. Me, I've seen the rushes. They are magnificent. I'm in a piece of Art. I *like* being in a piece of Art. It gives me self-respect. It gives me a reason to be here. It tells me I made the right choice. Hell, it tells me I *made* a choice.

So when The Mule approaches me in the pub one night and asks me to join him and some friends for a drink, I decide it would be churlish not to. The Mule is big. He's helping us with locations, local crew, transport. 'You were in *Bad Boy Bubby*, weren't you?' he asks. 'That film is the town's favourite. We show it a lot. There's some people here who'd be honoured if you joined them.'

Bad Boy Bubby. Lightning Ridge. It makes sense. What's the point in fighting it?

The Mule has a table outside. I sit between him and Johnno's wife. Johnno sits across from me, beside another woman. They shake my hand. Johnno is small and wiry, with skin that is sun-wrinkled and hands that are larger than his frame would suggest. He wears a singlet and shorts. His wife has that peculiarly Australian outback look. Something slightly harsh in the features, with a permed hairdo and a floral dress highlighting a strict, thin-lined make-up regime. I know this look. I grew up with it. Wrong skin in the wrong climate.

Johnno and The Mule offer me a special drink, something they make down in the mines. 'Down in the mines?' I ask.

'Well,' they explain, 'distilling your own drink, you know, it's not legal. Not this stuff, at any rate. But the police turn a blind eye to what you do in your own mine. They wouldn't last long if they didn't!' They laugh. 'It's just gentle,' they continue, 'nothing strong. Would you like some?'

'Why not?' I answer.

The effect is instantaneous. For a while I wonder if I've been drugged. I have a sense of panic. The verandah doesn't spin, it shakes, like being on a boat, and sound and vision alternately grow and diminish. 'Good, isn't it?' says The Mule, who doesn't seem to be affected. In fact, no one else does. I don't want to let on that I am, so I agree. Johnno turns to me.

'Your film, mate, *Bubby*. That was a real film. That was a real Aussie film about a real Aussie family. Blew me out.'

His wife agrees. 'Real Aussie film about a real Aussie family,' she repeats. 'Why don't they make more films like that?'

I laugh. I think they're joking. Bubby's mother was abusive, she locked him up for 35 years, had an incestuous relationship with him, beat and mistreated him. The family set-up is hardly typical. Mr and Mrs Johnno have to be joking.

They're not. Their faces are grim. The effect of the drink hasn't worn off and I don't understand what's happening here. 'Sorry,' I explain, 'I just didn't expect you to say that.' Johnno hasn't taken his eyes off me.

'Have you heard of Poh Pia?' he asks. I'm still caught between hilarity, fear and mental incoherence, but the look on his face warns me not to say I thought Poh Pia was a Malaysian food. 'Poh Pia was my dad,' Johnno continues. 'He died recently. Biggest party the town's seen. He used to keep my brother and me in a cage at night, haul us up into the loft. Sometimes he'd drag us out, keep us in a half-nelson while he did things. To my mum and stuff. Then he'd put us back. That's what I mean, mate. I saw your film, and I cried. Real Australian film about a real Australian family.'

The people around the table are nodding. I don't know if this is a hoax. Whatever is in the drink is still going, and I'm getting scared. What's the right response? Is this a true story or is it a set-up? Am I going to end up down a mine regardless of what I say? Have they heard I'm playing an incestuous paedophile and are out to get me? It doesn't look that way, they're all looking at the table and nodding, except for Johnno's wife who's patting his arm. No one is looking at me now, it's not the way violent set-ups usually work, but who's to tell? In any case, I still don't know what to say.

Another man joins us. Tall, brown-skinned, long hair, singlet and jeans dusty from a mine. Johnno introduces us. We shake hands and it hurts. 'This bloke,' Johnno tells the newcomer, 'is Bad Boy Bubby!' The new guy doesn't know what that means. Johnno explains: 'The film *Bad Boy Bubby*, this bloke was the actor! He's a star, mate, a star.'

'So what?' says the new guy. 'Whatta ya want me to do, fight him?' and he stands up.

This is it, I think, this is the set-up. 'Hey,' I say, 'I don't want to fight anyone.'

The new guy sits down. 'I'll fight him if you want me to,' he tells Johnno. But Johnno doesn't want him to. Johnno's truly affected. The film did something for him. Bubby in the flesh ain't the same, but he wants it to be. And he wants everyone to know.

I retreat back to the motel room. What's happening to Johnno is beyond me. I look at the holes in the plasterboard ceiling. All those holes in all that plasterboard. It's really ugly. I think of the promise of Venice and what everyone said. I've heard that Toni Collette's Bruce Willis film, *The Sixth Sense*, is huge. That's the sort of transformed reality I'd dreamt of over in Venice. Not Wild West Australia. I'd rather be in a luxury suite with a spa and room service and cable TV. I'd much rather be getting paid $25 million than $25,000. I'd rather have flown here first class. I'd love to have my name in huge letters, with a deep American voice saying, 'With Academy Award-winner Nicholas Hope.' I'd like so much. It seems such a tantalisingly small step to get there. I just don't know which step it is, or whether I'd have the energy, motivation, or even recognition to take it. And then, that picture of Johnno nodding at the table, trying to confront his past. That's big. I was part of it.

The drink or the drug is still swimming in my head, the holes in the ceiling are expanding and contracting. Someone knocks on the door. It's Jeff. Some of the crew are driving out to the hot springs, do I want to come? Hell yes. I didn't know there were hot springs here.

The two small, steaming pools are a 20-minute drive out of town. The water is so hot, it takes a while to acclimatise. We sit up to our necks, skin rapidly turning lobster pink. The water bubbles between our toes, up and around our bodies. There is tiling around the edge, so we rest our heads on it to look up at the night. There are few lights to counter the stars. They float like a gas in the sky, completely covering our vision.

I am in the desert, in a hot spring, looking at a sky filled with countless stars twinkling like fairyland. The polar opposite of Berlevåg. I used to be a bank clerk in Whyalla. It's becoming a mantra. I'd like to be a millionaire in a clever blockbuster film with celebrity parties and lavish excess and a lifetime's financial security, but there's something about the fringe moments.

I ring Bianca in her office. She is writing well, she tells me, the view from the window helps. The snow has come early in Norway. It's quite beautiful, she says. The stars shine off it. I tell her about the hot springs and the sky and the wig to make me young and the wig to make me old, the fabulous rushes and the violence and the mines and the craters and the white clay and the storms and Johnno and The Mule and the drug drink and . . .

'Wow,' she says. 'That's amazing. You used to be a bank clerk in Whyalla.'

epilogue

Scooby Doo, Queensland

'Y'ever tried that? Man, it'll blow y'r head, like, total. Y'know? Y'ever tried that?'

Rowan Atkinson, cornered, shakes his head politely. The other man, Someone Someone Junior, continues, 'Y'get a polaroid, y'know, like, of you and, like, me, man, it'll blow y'r . . . and y', y'know, y'cut 'em in half, man, and put them together? Freaky! FREAKY!! MAN!! You should TRY it! It'll BLOW y'r MIND!!' He jigs up and down a bit, in excitement. Mr Atkinson nods sympathetically. The female lead, who is romantically attached to the male lead, turns to her partner worriedly, and says, 'Honey, we can't do that, can we? I might look ugly if we did that. You might leave me. Would you leave me if we did that and I looked ugly? We can't do that, can we?' Her lover reassures her, 'I won't leave you, honey, you'll never be ugly to me.'

This is It. Hollywood in Australia. Big budgets, big stars,

big money. I have a tiny role, but it will take six days to film, and I get $5000 a day – cheap compared with others on $500,000 a day, but I'm not complaining. I get covered in prosthetics, I get to be grumpy and ham it up, this is playing not acting and who cares anyway, it's *Scooby Doo*, for God's sake, it was a bad cartoon in the first place. Five thousand dollars a day is silly money.

The stars are cosseted. Young things who have been famous since birth, whose conversations are about film sets and hotel rooms, whose demeanours are teenage and whose salaries are obscene. They are Good People, I am told, you can talk to them, like, normal. You know? Like, they're normal!

What we are doing today should have been done yesterday, but a member of the paparazzi created a problem. He took photographs of the two romantically linked leads, who then retreated to their mansion and refused to come out until the photographer was removed from the island. Since he had every right to be there, this took some time. One of the producers rang the production manager to say he couldn't believe tourists were still allowed on the island, the company had spent enough money on filming rights, shit they should have the whole fucking army at their disposal! In fact, why couldn't they get the fucking army? Somehow they found a loophole that allowed the film to exclude the photographer from taking any more photos, somehow they found a way to escort him off the island under armed guard, but by then the sun had gone down and a whole day's filming had been lost and all the extras had to be held for another day and the company had just lost another million or so US dollars.

I'd put my little chair in the middle of all the stars' big chairs, and written my name in chalk to compete with all their embossed ones. I sat in it, watching the bikini-clad extras who were waiting to see if the stars would come out. Someone Someone Junior was creating a fuss because he hadn't got an embossed chair, and an assistant director found him an unembossed one and wrote his name on it in chalk as well. We were comrades now. 'Man, I caint beLIEVE this!' he said. I nodded. It did seem an extreme reaction, the stars were being paid millions, paparazzi were irksome but this was just a couple of photos, there was no need to hold up the filming. 'They should just beat the fucker up and throw him to the SHARKS, man!'

I was having a good time. The longer the stars didn't shine, the more lots of $5000 I'd get.

'Ah well,' I said, 'that's Hollywood.'

I sat in my chair in the sun and watched the bikini-clad extras. They were practising running towards the esplanade as two helicopters and a speedboat arrived on cue; it all had to be coordinated with the three cameras. The scene was being rehearsed just in case the stars changed their minds.

The bikini extras finished their rehearsal and spread out on the grass in front of me. This was *very* Hollywood. The stars hadn't emerged from their mansion and wouldn't until after sunset. The producers were on their telephones arranging for extras, helicopters and speedboats to be available for an extra day, and for more security staff, with dogs, to be hired for all the leads. The rest of their time here would be under guard. An assistant director came over, asked me if I wanted anything.

I was sitting in my little chair, and I was enjoying myself. It wasn't where I wanted to be forever, I knew that now, but it was fine for a visit. I looked up at him, and I smiled.

postscript

Ten Years On

A man who claims he is always mistaken for Pat Rafter is frothing at the mouth, choking on his beer, coughing out the words 'Sorry, mate' as he sprays the table with flecks of pepper, beer and spittle. My brother is staring at him in horror. 'Sorry, mate, sorry,' Pat Rafter's clone says again, as he empties the rest of the pepper mill into his mouth. His eyes are streaming now. He chokes again and sneezes over our drinks, gulps some beer and froths even more. 'So what *is* your name?' he splutters.

My brother hasn't seen this kind of public behaviour before. He's been living in Japan for 14 years – people could get certified for this kind of thing there. He's been away for the whole cult phenomenon I've been through. I explain that the man is trying to be friendly, it's his way of trying to endear himself, it's a little extreme and rude but it's not out of the ordinary. 'Yes it is,' replies my brother.

Pat Rafter's clone is settling now, the pepper has run its course. 'Come on, mate, what's your name? Hey! Hey!' he grabs a passing girl. 'Hey! Have you seen that movie *Bad Boy Bubby*? What was the guy's name? The guy who was in it, do you remember? Look, this is him! What's his name?'

My brother and I are out for a drink in a Surry Hills hotel in Sydney on a Sunday afternoon. We are here because of the jazz band. I don't like jazz, but my brother does, and the band are all old codgers. My brother says it makes a change from the usual bright, young, brittle scene offered by the rest of Sydney. He has only been back for a week. He is suffering culture shock. So many overweight people, he says, so many illiterates, so much senseless, inflated egotism, so much brashness. We were trying to talk in between the band's sets of music when Pat's clone came over and sat with us, interrupting our conversation. Just a friendly gesture, he explained, it's the Australian way. 'I thought you were Hugo Weaving,' he says, 'but you weren't. That's okay, I'm always mistaken for Pat Rafter! Yeah, *Bubby*'s the only film Hugo hasn't done . . . Woah, shit, that's the wrong thing to say. Look, watch this!' and he unscrewed the lid from the pepper mill and poured half the contents in his mouth. 'Man, I'm sorry,' he choked as his eyes began to stream.

We don't stay. You can't. They either want to be your best friend or they want to fight you, and neither is very attractive. They want to parade you as something special, but they also want to let you know you're not. 'Does this kind of thing happen a lot?' my brother asks. At first I think he means being mistaken for Hugo, which happens, but not that much any more, but then I realise he means the insane proprietorial intrusions into personal space and time.

'Often enough,' I answer. He looks at me questioningly. A little suspiciously, I think.

'Don't you find it intrusive?'

Sometimes. Ten years of being recognised for the same thing is on the edge. It's about time it was something else. Sometimes it is, and then intrusive doesn't come into it. Gratifying does. Preening does. Coquettishness, even. It may be intrusive, but by golly it still feeds your ego and you're the one being admired, and even if you have to leave like we had to leave, you have to leave because they've endowed you with some glory they think they don't have. It's a small, tenuous, pathetic claim to individuality and specialness, but it's mine.

'It's intrusive when they're loonies,' I answer. I'm thinking of the woman who followed Bianca and me home from a film screening, then stood outside the door shouting obscenities about actors who stalk young girls. Or the man at the Haugesund Film Festival in Norway who had seen *Bubby* 13 times and knew Bianca was star-fucking for money: he told her so while he held me up against a wall because he had questions about the film he wanted answered. He started screaming a quote from the film – 'Fuck you, God!' – as the security guards started to peel his hands off me. He could still be heard as they dragged him backwards out of the venue. And now the pepper-eating, mouth-frothing Pat Rafter clone. But that's not the whole of it. It's a complex, accidental form of intrusion. It takes time to mature. And it's married to so many other things, you wouldn't want to let go of it.

We go to meet Bianca for dinner. She's finished the first draft of her new script ahead of time. She'll be going back to Norway soon, to follow up on it and work for another production company as an in-house writer. She'll find a place for us to live before I follow. I might go through the United States to meet up with the Warner Brothers woman, who is now in Texas writing a film about men on death row, which she wants me to be in. A death-row man. She hasn't told me the crime yet.

I'm thinking of putting a showreel together of all the potentially psychopathic moments I have done, and all the dying moments, and presenting myself to the Americans as Cheap Psychopath. In Hollywood, all psychopaths have to die, and die well. Maybe that actor in Adelaide was right: it's all a case of cornering your market. I could be Hollywood Psychopath and Edges of the World Weirdo. Look at Kevin Spacey, it worked for him. *Seven* catapulted him along, but let's not dwell on that.

Meanwhile, rehearsals are about to start in Sydney on the Norwegian play *Elling*, a comedy sent to me by the scriptwriter. I get to play Elling, an anally obsessive man who has just been released from a mental institution and has to come to terms with the new world he is entering. It's a co-op play, which means we won't get paid, but we will share the profits from the 18-day season in the 90-seat theatre. In Hollywood, the Americans are doing a remake of the film of the play of the book, and Kevin Spacey will play Elling. Small world. Maybe he will get to have a share of the profits of his venture, too.

There's a line *my* character, Elling, says when talking about the repulsion, and attraction, of the world his best friend sees and wants to inhabit: 'It's an odd form of reality, but it is reality, nonetheless.'

Not so odd.

A long way from Whyalla – but I can still make out the blasted remains of Mount Laura.

acknowledgements

I would love to claim this book as mine, all mine . . . but as always, many people deserve thanks for their support, encouragement and involvement. And, as always, too many to mention. Some, however, are at the top of the list.

Very special thanks to Anna, Bianca, Cath, all my family, Garth, Julietta, Michael, Rolf and Tim.

And thanks to everybody mentioned in the book. If you missed out, there's always the chance of a sequel.

Thanks also to Fran, my literary agent from Curtis Brown Australia, Fiona, my Random House publisher, and Sophie, my Random House editor, who helped create a book from a manuscript. And to James Laurie Management in Australia, and Maureen and Thea from Peters Fraser and Dunlop, UK, for making it possible for me to write 'Actor' in the occupation section of various forms . . .